Thinking Together

A programme of activities for developing thinking skills at KS2

by Lyn Dawes, Neil Mercer and Rupert Wegerif

Q
QUESTIONS
PUBLISHING
COMPANY

THE *QUESTIONS* PUBLISHING COMPANY LTD
BIRMINGHAM
2000

First published in 2000
by The Questions Publishing Company Ltd
27 Frederick Street, Birmingham B1 3HH

© 2000 Lyn Dawes, Neil Mercer and Rupert Wegerif

Edited by Juliet Sutton
Designed by Al Stewart
Illustrations by Martin Cater
Cover design by Arlene Adams

ISBN: 1-84190-035-4

Contents

How and why to teach the Thinking Together *lessons*

The aims of *Thinking Together*   3
The *Thinking Together* approach   4
Making the most of group work   5
Improving the quality of talk   6
Working with ICT   7
Assessment   8
Thinking Together lessons and curriculum requirements   13
Evaluation   14

Section A Focus on talk

Teachers' notes   19
Lesson 1 Talk about talk   22
Lesson 2 Talking in groups   28
Lesson 3 Deciding on ground rules   33
Lesson 4 Using the ground rules   41
Lesson 5 Reasoning with the ground rules   46

Section B Talking, thinking and learning

Teachers' notes   55
Lesson 6 Persuasion   57
Lesson 7 Kate's choice   61
Lesson 8 Who pays?   65
Lesson 9 Water voles   74
Lesson 10 Town plan   90
Lesson 11 A fair test   95
Lesson 12 Non-fiction   98
Lesson 13 Looking into poems   104
Lesson 14 Staying friends   108
Lesson 15 Strategy   113
Lesson 16 Making a meaning web   116
More information about *Thinking Together*   121

How and why to teach the *Thinking Together* lessons

The aims of *Thinking Together*

The *Thinking Together* book of materials is designed to develop the language and reasoning skills of children aged eight to eleven (KS2), and help improve their educational achievement across the curriculum subjects. Activities are included which have relevance to English, mathematics, science and citizenship.

The overall aim of *Thinking Together* is to improve children's use of language for thinking critically and constructively. The activities are organised into a series of Talk Lessons.

This book is linked to the *Thinking Together* website which extends the programme with further information on the *Thinking Together* approach. The site can be found at this address:

http://www.thinkingtogether.org.uk

For teachers

The materials are a means of organising whole-class and group activities, in ways that have been shown to improve the quality of children's educational performance and their participation in class.

For children

The activities will:

- Help the children to communicate more effectively within a group.
- Improve their ability to reason, both together and on their own.
- Raise their self-awareness and awareness of others, by providing opportunities for them to share and debate ideas in fair and supportive ways.
- Provide the communication skills that they need to use ICT as a tool to support their own learning.

The aims and themes of the Talk Lessons are closely related to curriculum requirements for primary schools. These links are shown on the table on page 11 of this book.

The *Thinking Together* approach

The *Thinking Together* approach is the result of applied research carried out over several years by a team based at the Open University. This research, which was supported by the Economic and Social Research Council and the Citizenship Foundation, showed that by using some practical, down-to-earth strategies and activities, teachers helped children to become better at communicating and reasoning together. It also showed that children were then able to apply these skills effectively in curriculum activities, particularly those involving computers. An additional finding of the research was that the children who took part in specific activities became better at tackling reasoning problems on their own. The research provided clear evidence of a link between the development of children's communication skills and the improvement of their critical thinking.

Most of this research was carried out in primary and middle schools in south-east England, where teachers worked closely with researchers in the development and testing of the activities in the programme. The findings have now been disseminated in many parts of the world, and have very recently been used to develop activities in Mexican schools. A list of publications, which report this research in detail, is provided on page 121 of this book. The text of some of these articles can be found on the *Thinking Together* website (http://wwwthinkingtogether.org.uk).

A key element of the *Thinking Together* approach is the concept of **exploratory talk**. Exploratory talk occurs when partners engage critically but constructively with each other's ideas. Relevant knowledge is shared, suggestions are sought and opinions offered for joint consideration. Ideas and suggestions may be challenged and counter-challenged, but challenges are justified with reasons. In exploratory talk, knowledge is made publicly accountable and reasoning becomes apparent in the talk.

When children are using language in this way, their reasoning becomes apparent in their speech, for example in the frequent use of words such as 'because' and 'why'. The ability to use language in this way is a valuable part of children's education – in adult life they will need to be able to use it effectively in work situations and in order to take an active role in society. However, when group work in some English primary classrooms was observed (at an early stage in the *Thinking Together* research) it was found that hardly any exploratory talk was occurring. Other research has shown that the quality of group work is frequently both unproductive and unsatisfactory, with pupils failing to understand how they are expected to work together. The *Thinking Together* materials were developed to help teachers improve this situation.

Making the most of group work

It is now widely recognised that achieving the best practice in education is not a matter of choice between whole-class (teacher-directed) or small-group (pupil-directed) teaching methods. Both these strategies for teaching and learning have their strengths and purposes, and effective teaching depends on maintaining a suitable balance between whole-class and group-based work. The Talk Lessons in this programme have been designed to help teachers achieve this balance.

Children may never have thought about how they talk together or considered whether different ways of communicating might make group activities more productive and enjoyable. They need help to learn how to use language effectively. As teachers, we may not have made our expectations sufficiently clear when we ask pupils to 'discuss' or 'talk together in a group'.

Group activity is more likely to be productive and fulfilling if based on the following ground rules:

- All relevant information is shared amongst the group.
- Assertions and opinions should be backed up by reasons.
- Suggestions and opinions can be challenged and discussed.
- Alternative options are considered before any decision is made. Each person in turn should be invited to speak.
- Everyone in the group should be encouraged to speak by the other members.
- The group should try to reach agreement.
- The group accepts collective responsibility for decisions made and any actions taken because of those decisions.

The exploratory talk not only generates more effective group activity; it can also help individual children to improve their 'critical thinking' or reasoning.

It is frequently the case that, without intervention, certain individuals may dominate group work. Some people find it easier to assert their points of view, and others working with them may find their ideas are ignored or dismissed, without good reason. The most confident and determined children may take over activities, so that their ideas are always accepted and used, whilst others, who may have more relevant ideas to offer, are rarely heard. The quiet child in a group often finds the whole experience frustrating, with no opportunities to express his or her ideas. Children like this may need to learn strategies to enable them to take a more active role, or be offered a more supportive environment in which they can develop the confidence to speak. On the other hand, an assertive child may really want to listen to the views of other members, but may simply lack good strategies for communicating with them.

Managing the talk groups

There are many factors to be taken into consideration when dividing the class into groups for each Talk Lesson. The following points are useful to note:

- 'Friendship' groups may not be ideal for Talk Lessons, as friends working together tend to agree with each other's suggestions, without critical consideration.
- Each talk group should include a child who can read and write reasonably well, so that any written instructions, or other materials, are properly understood. The designated child should be informed of this special responsibility. The lessons are designed so that children of different literacy abilities can contribute on an equal footing.
- Mixed gender groups allow greater opportunity for developing children's co-operative and communicative abilities.
- The talk groups work best where they consist of three children of mixed ability, including both sexes, and at least one child who may be likely to encourage more reluctant individuals to participate.

Improving the quality of talk

This programme is organised into Talk Lessons, which enable children to learn and practise ways of using language as a tool for thinking together. As a result, children will increasingly begin to use language for thinking together, or co-reasoning. They will also begin to use more exploratory talk, which is an effective means of communicating in a group, involving principles of critical and constructive thinking. Thinking together, out loud, is good preparation for thinking alone.

In each Talk Lesson, the teacher sets up a situation in which children must solve problems together. The lessons give children a clear structure for their work together, with ways of using language that they can all understand and apply. Through the first few lessons, the children are guided towards formulating some straightforward ground rules for talking together. If followed, these rules ensure that all voices are heard and all points of view are supported by reasons. All members of a group are expected to seek agreement before taking a decision. This means that no individual can be made to feel responsible for a wrong group decision, and there is shared 'glory' when things turn out right.

Working with ICT

ICT activities can be found on the *Thinking Together* website. Computers offer access to so much information and experience that children can be overwhelmed. The challenge for teachers is to organise computer-based activities that will help children to convert this information and experience into knowledge. One effective way to facilitate this process is to encourage pupils to discuss information with each other. When participating in discussions, children are prompted to explain and justify ideas, which results in a clearer understanding. They may also absorb new ideas and concepts which may otherwise have passed them by. When children are tackling problems presented on the computer, successful learning is more likely to occur when they sit back from the screen and discuss the problem in their groups before making a response. Interacting with computers can be very absorbing. It is worth reminding children that they are expected to talk together before they start, and ask them to read or rehearse their ground rules for talk. Groups of three can work well around a computer screen but you may need to sort out seating and turn-taking with the mouse or keyboard before the task begins.

The three-part structure of the Talk Lessons, in which the teacher introduces aims at the beginning and then returns to them during the whole-class plenary session at the end, is an effective way of integrating computer activities into the curriculum. The aim of the talk group's discussion is then made explicit in the lesson aims, and the plenary session enables children to decide whether they have achieved those aims. Through this process, children become aware that their talk together at the computer can make an important contribution to their learning. Children can concentrate on discussing issues, ideas and decisions, knowing that this will achieve their aim, regardless of whether they 'win the game' or are the person to 'click the mouse'.

Useful teaching strategies

Trials of the Talk Lessons in schools have shown that the best results are usually obtained by teachers who:

- Make the aims for each lesson clear.
- Remind children regularly to use their ground rules for talk, once these have been agreed (as part of Lesson 3).
- Model the type of language the children should be using with each other; for example, encourage them to reason and reflect, by asking 'why' and 'how' questions.
- Use questioning, not only as a test of pupils' knowledge, but also to lead them through a line of reasoning, with a series of related questions.
- Help children to recognise and value the language and reasoning skills they are developing, by asking them to consider whether using the ground rules has improved the ways in which they talk and work together.
- Review the aims at the end of each Talk Lesson, which helps consolidate children's learning.

Assessment

The Open University research team made video recordings of children working in groups and transcribed their talk to observe how their use of language changed over time, and how they used talk to solve problems and learn together. This method may be difficult for teachers to use, but there are other methods that are easier, for example:

Self-assessment by the child

Keeping a *Thinking Together* diary helps to build up a picture of the child's talking, listening and reasoning activities over a finite length of time. This method of self-assessment is straightforward for both teacher and child to use and interpret. Adding to the content of the diary should be done quickly and regularly, in the same way that children update their reading records. A comprehensive *Thinking Together* diary can fulfil several purposes:

- It can provide an overview of the range of opportunities for thinking together which the child has experienced.
- It can record the child's strengths and weaknesses in thinking together with others.

- It can focus the attention of the child and the teacher on talking, listening and thinking together, ensuring these activities are valued.
- It can act as an informal and ongoing assessment of talking, listening and thinking.
- It can enable the planning of activities to take place.
- It can provide a resource for reporting the child's achievements.

Overleaf is an example of a *Thinking Together* diary. This diary is designed for children to fill in themselves at the end of the week, and the teacher can add any comments or notes that s/he feels are necessary.

Thinking Together diary

Name:	Starting date:		
	Comment and date:	*Comment and date:*	*Comment and date:*
I talked in a group:			
I asked a question·			
I answered a question:			
I gave a reason:			
We used the ground rules:			
We thought of several different ideas:			
We made a group decision:			
The talk helped me change my mind:			
We fell out:			
The talk helped me to think of new ideas:			
We talked about everyone's ideas:			
I thought of some useful information and shared it with my group:			
I could not join in with the talk:			
Everyone shouted and didn't listen:			
I enjoyed the discussion:			
I found it difficult to talk in a group:			

Teacher assessment

It is not easy to give each child in a class the amount of attention that a teacher might wish. For this reason, it is useful to consider the range of assessment opportunities available, and different ways of recording evidence. The *Thinking Together* diary gives the child a chance to consider and record their own talking and their own thinking. Teacher assessment might begin with the teacher writing a short account of the child as a talking, listening and thinking person.

Below is a list of questions about an individual child's behaviour, during group discussions. It could be used as a checklist on a single occasion, or to build up a tally chart to show frequency of use over a longer time.

What am I looking for in the child's talk?

1. Does the child initiate and carry on conversations?
2. Does the child listen carefully?
3. Can the child's talk be easily understood?
4. Can the child describe experiences?
5. Can the child give instructions?
6. Can the child follow verbal instructions?
7. Does the child modify talk for different audiences?
8. Does the child ask questions?
9. Does the child give reasons?
10. Does the child ask others for their views?
11. Does the child reply to challenging questions with reasons?
12. Can the child take joint responsibility for decisions?
13. Can the child 'think aloud'?
14. Can the child generate and consider an alternative point of view?

This list could be made much more detailed. For example, the question 'Does the child listen carefully' could be turned into the following list:

Does the child listen carefully:
- to a familiar adult;
- to an unfamiliar adult;
- to friends;
- to unfamiliar children;
- when working in a group;
- in a whole class situation;
- in a whole school situation?

The other questions could also be given more detail, if necessary. The assessment may be an initial overview, an ongoing monitoring of progress, or a detailed study in order to support an application for a statement of special needs in education. Different purposes require different sorts of assessment, and only the teacher can decide what best suits that purpose. An example of a simple monitoring chart might look this:

Class speaking and listening monitoring chart

Child's name	Date	Talk context	Note:

Thinking Together lessons and curriculum requirements

Links with the National Curriculum are summarised in the table below. In addition, Lessons 6: *Persuasion*, 12: *Non-fiction* and 13: *Looking into poems* are designed to integrate with the National Literacy Strategy.

	Programmes of study	Lesson in this pack
English 1 (speaking and listening)	1a-f; 2a-e; 3a-f 4a-d 6a-c 9c	All lessons 8, 14, 15 1, 6, 16 2
English 2 (reading)	2a-d; 3c; 5a-e 4a-e	12 13
Maths (Ma3)	1b-e, h	5A, 7, 15
Science 1 (investigative)	1a,b; 2a-d	11
Science 2 (living things)	5a-c	9
Science 3 (materials)	1a; 2a, d, f	11
Science 4 (physical processes)	2c	12
Geography	1d; 5a,b 1a-e; 2a, c, e, g; 3c; 4; 6d, e	9 10
ICT	2c; 4b 1a-c; 2a; 3a, b; 4a-c	7 16
PSHE/Citizenship	1a; 2d-f; 4a; 5g 1a; 2a-f; 4a-f; 5g	4 7, 8, 14

For teachers in Scotland:
Guidance on how the *Thinking Together* programme relates to the requirements of the Scottish Curriculum can be found on the *Thinking Together* website http://www.thinkingtogether.org.uk

Evaluation

At the end of the series of Talk Lessons, you might wish to carry out a summary evaluation, both of the lessons and the progress that the children have made. The children's *Thinking Together* diaries and your assessment of each child's development will provide some information. Additional information can be gained by discussing the Talk Lessons with the children.

- Did the children enjoy the lessons?
- Which lessons were their favourites?
- What do they feel they have learned?
- Can they see how this knowledge could be used in school, or at home?
- Have they noticed other people reasoning together? e.g. at school; at home; on television programmes; using computers, etc.

Alternatively, ask the groups to compile a short talk, which puts forward their opinions of both the lessons, and their own learning. This could be presented to the class.

A structure for more lessons

The Talk Lessons format can be used as a structure for lessons across the curriculum. Its main features are summarised here:

A lesson plan format for *Thinking Together* lessons

Lesson number ____

Resources

Aims

(These should be made explicit at the start of the lesson.)

Introduction

Explain the lesson aims, and give instructions for the group work.

Group work

Children work collaboratively on tasks in their groups.

Plenary

Restate the lesson aims and discuss whether children feel that these have been achieved.

Follow-up work

The emphasis should always be on stating the lesson aims, especially if aims are to do with talking and reasoning, which in other circumstances may not be given a high priority, particularly where children are being asked to complete written work, art work, or computer-based tasks.

Section A
Focus on talk

Teachers' notes

Thinking Together is intended as an approach to teaching and learning as well as a set of specific activities. The detailed Talk Lesson plans included here have been tried and tested in classrooms and provide a range of useful activities for teaching talking and listening skills. However, these lessons also develop thinking skills, which have the potential to raise levels of achievement. The benefits of these activities on educational progress are most noticeable where children are explicitly encouraged to use ground rules for effective talk as the basis for group-work in all curriculum areas. The lessons suggested here are examples of the *Thinking Together* approach which may inspire you to make your own adaptations and to develop the approach throughout the curriculum. The Talk Lessons are divided into two sections:

Focus on talk

The first five lessons, collectively called *Section A: Focus on talk*, aim to encourage children to become more aware of the ways in which they talk together. Pupils are given the task of establishing specific ground rules for talk. Each lesson focuses on a different ground rule or sub-component of effective *Thinking Together*, for example, accurate listening, asking questions or giving reasons. These lessons could be used in the first week of a new school year to create a climate of collaborative learning in the classroom, or perhaps to start a new term with a new approach.

Talking, thinking and learning

The second set of lessons (Lessons 6 to 16) are called *Section B: Talking, thinking and learning*. These lessons are intended to build on the (already established) ground rules and allow children to apply them to different areas of the curriculum. It is assumed in each lesson that the children know how to use the ground rules in order to think together effectively. However, some of the lessons in this section revisit the aims of *Focus on talk*, to reinforce certain ground rules. It is important that pupils complete all of the lessons in the first section, before progressing further.

The following Talk Lessons are designed to teach ground rules for encouraging exploratory talk. All of the lessons in this section should be completed before moving on to the next session. In Section B, it will be assumed that the class has agreed on a set of ground rules for talking together, which will be displayed prominently in the classroom, and referred to frequently.

These lesson plans can be used as a template for developing further lessons and suggestions of how to do this are included, along with photocopiable worksheets.

Each Talk Lesson plan has the following structure:

Resources

Materials needed for each activity are listed here, including the photocopiable activity sheets contained in this book.

Aims

One critical aspect of the Talk Lessons is that, as each lesson starts, the teacher explains the lesson aims to the children. This helps to establish a shared purpose for each activity, and keeps the focus firmly on the talk. Any reading, writing or drawing the children may do is incidental. Pupils should be aware that they must concentrate their greatest efforts on the way in which they talk to one another.

Introduction

Each lesson begins with a whole class session, in which the teacher explains the lesson aims, talks about the main themes with the class and sets up any activities. The introduction notes are intended for teachers' use, rather than pupils, and are therefore not written in 'child-friendly' language.

Group work

During this phase the teacher asks pupils to sit in their designated 'talk groups'. The pupils will then work collaboratively on tasks in these groups.

Plenary

The teacher brings the class together at the end of the lesson in order to:

- enable groups to share their work with the class;
- lead a class discussion, drawing out the main points that have emerged;
- review the lesson aims, allowing the class to decide whether they have been fulfilled.

This discussion can also be used, by teacher and pupils, as a means of informal assessment.

Follow-up work

Some of the lessons include extra activities for the children to work on, either independently at the end of the lesson, or at home. There may also be suggestions for further lessons or reinforcement activities.

The five lessons in Section A are:

Lesson 1: Talk about talk
Lesson 2: Talking in groups
Lesson 3: Deciding on ground rules
Lesson 4: Using the ground rules
Lesson 5: Reasoning with the ground rules

Talk about talk

Resources
Dictionaries, thesaurus, display materials, *Worksheets 1A: A list of talk words, 1B: Sorting talk, 1C: Speech bubbles.*

Aims
To raise children's awareness of how they talk. To introduce some words for describing ways of talking and enable children to practise using them.

Introduction
Introduce the new 'talk topic' and explain the aims for Lesson 1. Ask the children for their ideas about talk, using the following open-ended questions as a structure. These questions should elicit a range of contributions based on personal experience and ideas.

General questions
Are you good at talking?
Do you ever get asked to stop talking – who asks this – when?
Does anyone ever try to make you talk when you don't want to?
Do you like using the telephone – who do you talk to?
Do you know anyone who is easy to talk to – can you say why?

Questions on learning to talk
Has anyone got a baby brother or sister at home?
How do babies learn to talk?
Who taught you how to talk?
Do you learn how to talk in school?

Questions on using talk
Are you asked to talk together in class?
In which lessons does this happen?
Why is talking is a useful skill? (Give reasons.)
What tasks can people get done by talking to each other?
How would you communicate with other people if you couldn't talk?
How many different languages can you speak?
How many different languages have you heard of?

Questions on communicating
What happens when people talk but others con't listen?
What are the differences between talking and writing?

Group work

1. *Sorting talk*
Provide each group of children with *Worksheet 1A: A list of talk words* and *Worksheet 1B: Sorting talk*. Ask the groups to talk together to put each word on *Worksheet 1A* into one of the boxes on *Worksheet 1B*. Tell them that they should:

▲ use a dictionary to clarify any unfamiliar words;
▲ only write the words in, once the group has agreed;
▲ find two new words to go into each box by using the thesaurus.

2. *Speech bubbles*
Provide each child with a copy of *Worksheet 1C: Speech bubbles*. Ask the group to:

▲ choose a word from the list on *Worksheet 1A*;
▲ draw a cartoon and a speech bubble in the first box, to show the word being used;
▲ write the word in the space below the cartoon;
▲ pass the sheet to another group member until everyone in the group has drawn a cartoon on each sheet.

3. *Display*
Ask each child to draw a life-sized talking head with a large speech bubble, then write one of the talking words in it. These can be mounted to make a display. Set up a class discussion for the children to share their completed work. Ask them to consider:

▲ When is it important to be silent?
▲ Why is silence important in some lessons?
▲ Do some people enjoy silence more than others?
▲ What has silence to do with thinking and concentrating?
▲ Can people talk and think at the same time?

Plenary

Review the lesson aims to check whether the children feel that these have been achieved.

Follow-up work

▲ At home, children could ask parents/relatives to describe their experiences in classrooms – when was talk allowed, encouraged, or discouraged?

▲ Children could find out how old they were when they began to talk, and see if anyone remembers what they first said, or recalls any amusing things that they said.

▲ Children who can speak more than one language should be asked to contribute by describing how they choose which language to use when they are talking. What problems have they encountered? What problems have single language speakers encountered in visiting other countries?

▲ Sign languages for the hearing impaired can be studied.

▲ Children can find out about codes for communicating, such as Morse code, semaphore, etc. Dance/ drama can be used to explain 'body language' – what are its limitations when compared to spoken language?

▲ If any of the class uses email to communicate with a friend, they could bring a printed sample to share. What are the similarities and differences between email, talking together, and writing to one another? Comics can provide a rich source of speech bubbles. In some, language is used creatively to convey sound or action. The class can draw cartoon characters with speech bubbles to convey the meaning of the words on *Worksheet 1A* for display.

A list of talk words

brag	reply
chat	tell
chatter	softly
conversation	stammer
demand	argue
dialogue	splutter
enquire	threaten
explain	screech
gossip	answer
laugh	natter
loudly	ask
moan	croak
mumble	grumble
mutter	dispute
persuade	reason
scream	request
shout	explain
tell off	row
whisper	fiercely
yell	discuss

Sorting talk

Talk **LOUDLY**

Talk

Talk quietly

Talk *angrily*

Question and answer

Any other words

Speech bubbles

Cartoon

Word

Cartoon

Word

Cartoon

Word

Cartoon

Word

Cartoon

Word

Cartoon

Word

Talking in groups

Resources
Paper and pens, stopwatch or timer, *Worksheet 2: Some starter questions*.

Aims
To start children working together in talk groups and establish group cohesion. To help children practise taking turns in talk.

Introduction
Explain the aims for Lesson 2 to the children. Talk to the children about the criteria used to organise the groups; explain that each group is a combination of these sorts of people:

- ▲ a good listener;
- ▲ a good writer;
- ▲ a person who has lots of good ideas;
- ▲ a co-operative person;
- ▲ a thoughtful person;
- ▲ a confident person.

Explain that this means that friends will not always be working together, that the groups have been carefully chosen, and that they are not negotiable. Hand out or display *Worksheet 2: Some starter questions*, and explain the task.

Group work

1. Interviewing
Two members of the group have to interview the third about their favourite free-time activity or hobby. Nothing at all should be written down by the group at this stage. Display the prompt questions and explain that these are only suggestions – their own ideas may well be better. The interview will last one minute. Interviewers must listen carefully to the answers. After the first interview, the process is repeated with the other members of the group. If someone claims they have no interests, they should be asked to describe, in great detail, what they did the previous evening or weekend.

2. *Class discussion*

When the interviews are complete, the group talks together and appoints a speaker. Taking turns, the speakers from each group briefly describe the hobbies of the group members. Individuals may be asked to answer questions from class members.

Next set up a class discussion, with the following suggested talking points:

▲ Why do you think teachers sometimes ask you to work in groups?
▲ Is it always easier to work with your friends?
▲ Do you like working in a group – why/why not?
▲ Who do you think is a good person to work in a group with and why?
▲ What do you think are good rules for working together in a group? (Briefly – this will be developed further in Lesson 3.)
▲ If your group is trying to decide something, for example if you are using the computer, and one person makes a suggestion, what should the other members of the group ask for, before the suggestion is accepted? (The aim here is to encourage children to recognise the need for a reason.)

Plenary

Repeat the lesson aims, and check the children feel that these have been achieved.

Follow-up work

▲ Children can interview someone at home, or an invited guest from another class, about their hobby. These interviews will help the children to become 'good listeners'.
▲ The children can create a display board depicting their hobby, with a brief description, or use a 'question-and-answer' format to explain the activity. The talking groups can each be given a folder in which group work will be collected. Group members can discuss how to decorate this in a way that reflects their various interests.
▲ The class can begin a collection from magazines, newspapers, etc. of pictures of people talking together: politicians; parents and children; children playing games or at the computer;

adults discussing things, etc., to create a display with captions. The uses and purposes of talking together can be stressed.

If you have time, and want to develop the skills of clear communication, Lesson 2A could be used in addition to Lesson 2.

Some starter questions

What do you like doing in your free time?

Where do you go to do that?

What started you doing that in the first place?

Do you need special equipment or clothes?

Is it an expensive hobby?

How long have you been doing this activity?

What do your family think of it?

Who do you do it with?

What do you hope to achieve?

Do you ever get fed up and want to stop?

Do you think other people in this class would like to do it too?

What else do you enjoy doing?

Building copies

Resources
2 matching sets of construction material for each group (e.g. Lego baseboard and 10 Lego pieces).

Aims
To help children to give accurate instructions and to ask relevant questions.

Introduction
Explain to the children the aims for Lesson 2A, then explain the following activity:

Group work
Two group members are to sit back-to-back. One of them will make a model or pattern with their set of construction materials. Once it is complete, their partner must ask for instructions on how to build an identical model. Instructions can only be given in response to questions asked. The third group member observes and can make suggestions, if the partners cannot resolve difficulties. Once models are copied successfully, the partners change tasks within the group.

Plenary
Ask the class to describe the sort of questions that provided useful information, and the sort of descriptions that were most accurate. Restate the lesson aims and discuss whether children feel that these have been achieved.

Follow up-work
A similar activity can take place using paper and pencil. One of the partners draws an object, then (without naming it) describes how to draw it.

Mathematical vocabulary for this sort of activity could be illustrated and displayed for use: left, right, angle, right-angle, arc, curve, cylinder, rectangle, rhombus, rotate, etc.

This activity could also be undertaken by talk partners, using email.

Deciding on ground rules

Resources
Dictionary, thesaurus, *Teacher information sheets 3A, B and C. Worksheet 3: Talking words.*

Aims
To raise children's awareness of group talk. To introduce relevant vocabulary. To decide on a shared set of ground rules for talk.

Introduction
Explain to the children the aims for Lesson 3. Briefly introduce the concept of 'ground rules' as basic rules to which everyone agrees. Use examples such as school rules; rules at the swimming pool; rules for car drivers; rules for a sport. Explain that in some joint activities, people need to discuss things, which makes a set of 'talk rules' necessary. Use *Teacher information sheet 3A: Are these useful rules?* Ask individual children to read the rules aloud, then ask the class to comment on whether each rule would encourage group discussion. Please do not provide groups with a printed copy of this sheet, since it may affect the creation of original rules.

Group work
1. *Talking words*
(10-minute activity) Provide each group of children with *Worksheet 3: Talking words*. Groups should use a dictionary or thesaurus to write sentences which clarify the meaning of the words.

2. *Creating rules*
This activity is one of the most important in the whole *Thinking Together* programme. Ensure that the children are aware of this.

Ask the class to think silently for a minute about all they have learned about ways to discuss things effectively when working with a group.

Now the children should talk together in their groups. The task is to decide on what they consider are the six most important rules that people talking in groups should follow. That is, they should create and agree on a list of six *ground rules for talk*. They should keep in mind that the aim of each rule is to encourage sharing of ideas, and joint decision-making. Encourage the children to provide reasons for their suggestions.

Plenary

(Please read *Teacher information sheet 3B* before the plenary.) The purpose of the plenary session is to share ideas, and to decide on a summary list of ground rules for talk. In a whole class discussion, ask each group to contribute one of their rules. Point out where groups have devised similar rules. Record rules in note form. Ask for further rules from each group until all new ideas are recorded. Using these notes, the class should now agree on their ground rules for talk. All members of the class must be encouraged to agree to use these rules when working together.

Tell the class that you will display a poster of the agreed ground rules for talk so that group members can remind one another of them. Individual copies could also be made.

It is important that the children fell a sense of ownership of the rules. They should also be encouraged to see that the rules work to allow everyone a fair hearing.

Restate the lesson aims and discuss whether children feel that these have been achieved.

Follow-up work

Each child can have a printed copy of the rules to take home for discussion with parents. Children can then be asked to consider which ground rules for talk they think are being followed in other situations, for example:

> friends talking together;
> people talking in a school assembly;
> talking in the cinema, during a film;
> talking in class, when the teacher is introducing a new topic;
> talking in a science or maths investigation;
> talking during an outdoor game;
> talking on the telephone;
> pupils talking to the head teacher;

pupils talking to a school visitor.

What are the differences between these rules and the class ground rules for talk? The children should have the opportunity to consider the value of the class ground rules as a 'fair' means of sharing information, ideas, and opinions, and as a way of trying to find out and understand other people's reasons.

Ask the children to collect an example of the ground rules in action, over the course of a week. They can write down the context and what was said, or just try to remember it, for example, collect some uses of the word 'because'; an example of someone giving a reason; or an example of someone asking another person's opinion.

Are these useful rules?

1. The best reader should make the decisions for everybody.

2. Ask everyone in turn for an opinion.

3. Ask for reasons why.

4. Be critical of the idea, not of the person who put it forward.

5. If people challenge your ideas, you can give reasons for them.

6. Choose as quickly as you can, and then get on with it.

7. Discuss all the alternatives before making a decision.

8. If a wrong decision is made, one person should take the blame.

9. If you hear a good reason, you should change your mind.

10. If you know something is important, keep it to yourself.

11. If you want to be heard, shout.

12. Stick your fingers in your ears and make up your own mind.

13. Make sure the group agrees after talking.

14. Make up your own mind straight away and stick to it.

15. Respect other people's ideas.

16. Groups should try to agree before making a decision.

17. The most talkative person should speak most.

18. The oldest person should start the discussion.

19. There should be a leader and the group should do what they say.

20. You should always agree with your friends.

21. All relevant information should be shared among the group.

22. Be prepared to change your mind – it shows that you have listened.

23. Look at, and listen to, the person who is talking.

24. If you don't like someone, make sure they don't get heard.

25. Who cares what happens? Whatever is OK.

Ground rules for talk

It is vital for the success of the Talk Lessons that each class agrees upon a set of ground rules for talk, which will encourage effective, reasoned exploratory talk. The crucial ground rules (written in 'adult terms') are as follows:

▲ All relevant information is shared amongst the group.
▲ Assertions and opinions should be backed up by reasons.
▲ Suggestions and opinions can be challenged and discussed.
▲ Alternative options are considered before any decision is made. Each person in turn should be invited to speak.
▲ Everyone in the group should be encouraged to speak by the other members.
▲ The group should try to reach agreement.
▲ The group accepts collective responsibility for decisions made and any actions taken because of those decisions.

These rules need to be converted into a clear and simple version, which the children can appreciate and follow. The ground rules should be distinguished from other rules for talk used in class, such as, 'Don't interrupt an adult', 'Don't use bad language' and 'Don't talk in assembly'. Although useful, this type of rule is not appropriate for sustaining purposeful and effective discussion amongst children, with a focus on reasoned argument and shared information.

It is important that each class feels a sense of ownership of, and commitment to, their set of ground rules. Three examples of ground rules produced by Year 5 classes, as displayed on their classroom walls, are included on sheet 3B (continued).

The *Thinking Together* website includes footage of a class lesson in which ground rules are being established (see page 122 for the website address).

Examples

Example 1: **Class 5D's ground rules for talk**

1. Discuss things together; that means: ask every one for their opinion; ask for reasons why;
2. Listen to whoever is talking.
3. Be prepared to change your mind.
4. Think before you speak.
5. Respect other people's ideas, don't just use your own.
6. Share all the ideas and information you have.
7. Make sure that the group agrees after talking.

Example 2: **Our ground rules for talk**

We have agreed:

1. to share ideas;
2. to give reasons;
3. to question ideas;
4. to consider;
5. to agree;
6. to involve everybody;
7. that everyone accepts responsibility.

Example 3: **Our talking rules**

1. We share our ideas and listen to each other.
2. We talk one at a time.
3. We respect each other's opinions.
4. We give reasons to explain our ideas.
5. If we disagree we ask 'why?'
6. We try to agree in the end.

Talking words

Look at the following words and tell each other what these words mean. Use them in a sentence, if it makes your explanation easier. If there is a word the group doesn't know, use a dictionary or thesaurus. Tick each word when you think your group can say what it means.

1. opinion
2. agreement
3. relevant
4. argument
5. assertion
6. alternatives
7. challenge
8. discussion
9. reason
10. critical
11. respect
12. information
13. idea
14. sharing
15. group

Using the ground rules

Resources
Worksheets 4A: Finding things (a short story) and *4B: Taking turns to speak and listen.*

Aims
To allow the groups to practise their use of the ground rules for talk in a structured context. To develop an understanding of personal morality.

Introduction
Explain the aims for Lesson 4 and ask the children to recall their ground rules. Tell the class that the groups are going to use the agreed ground rules to come to some decisions together.

Distribute *Worksheet 4B* and ask each group's most adept reader to be responsible for reading it out. The children must read through the worksheet together, before they hear the story. Next, the teacher (or a fluent reader) should read the short story 'Finding things' aloud, from *Worksheet 4A*.

Group work
Ask the groups to follow the instructions on *Worksheet 4B*.

Plenary
Groups can contribute their ideas (contained in their answers to the worksheet questions) to a class discussion about the story. Groups could also talk about their use of the ground rules:
Was it possible to use the rules?
Was it difficult to use the rules?
What sort of problems arose?
What were the advantages of trying to stick to the rules?

Restate the lesson aims and discuss whether children feel that these have been achieved.

Follow-up work

▲ Each group could discuss and write an ending to the story.

▲ Groups could act out just their chosen 'ending' or the whole story, including the ending.

▲ The class could discuss the citizenship issues raised by the story: friendship, stealing, ownership and making difficult choices.

▲ The structured format of *Worksheet 4B* could be used to:
discuss issues raised in other stories;
undertake a joint problem-solving activity;
organise work together at the computer;
plan an investigation.

Finding things

Class 5 were doing maths. Tanya liked the sort of maths she was doing. She had to use her ruler to measure the sides of a rectangle, then add up all four numbers to find out what the perimeter measured altogether. She liked it because you could check if your adding up was right by measuring all the way round the rectangle. She was looking forward to moving on to bigger things, using the long tape measure - round the desk, round the carpet or round her friend Sam. Tanya was using a ruler Sam had given her for her birthday. It wasn't very long, only 20 cm, but it was special because it had a picture of a tiger on it. Sam came back to the table and sat down. Sam's work seemed to have a lot of red pen on it.
"Oh dear," said Sam.
"Tanya, please bring me your work to mark," said Mrs Smith.

Isaac was drawing triangles. He didn't really like maths, but he was trying his hardest to draw the lines accurately. He was using a school ruler, and it had little notches all down each side. 'Somebody's used this as a hammer!' thought Isaac. He carried on trying. He had £1.25 on the desk in front of him, and he kept looking at the coins and rearranging them. This was Isaac's dinner money. Usually Mum could only give him £1.00, but today he was lucky, and he was planning to buy a can of fizzy orange as a treat. As Tanya went past him to the teacher's desk, Isaac saw something fall on to the floor. It was a ruler. It was quite short, but it had perfectly straight edges. 'Just what I need,' thought Isaac. 'I bet I can use that to do my triangles really well. Then Mum will be pleased when she comes to parents' evening.' He picked up the ruler and drew a beautiful triangle with perfectly straight edges. "Wow!" said Jo who was sitting next to him. "Cool ruler."

Then the bell went and everyone started packing up for break. "Out you go!" said Mrs Smith.

It was a warm day, so Sam and Tanya didn't stop to get their coats. They ran straight outside. The playground filled up with people. After ten minutes of running around, Sam and Tanya drifted back towards the door. The bell would ring soon. "Hey!" said Tanya. "Look . . . there on the window-sill." She ran over to the school building. Outside, on the window-sill, was some money. Sam looked around. "Nobody about . . . I wonder who it belongs to?" "I don't know." said Tanya. There was a pound coin, a twenty pence and five one-penny pieces. "Well, you found it, so it's yours." said Sam. "You can share it with me . . . we'll buy some crisps on the way home." "I don't know." said Tanya, again. The bell rang. She scooped up the money and put it into her pocket. She promised herself that she would think about it later.

The class divided into groups for computer work and art. Tanya and Sam went to art, where they were drawing pictures of a Greek temple. "I need my ruler," said Tanya to the teacher, "can I go and get it?" "Yes . . . don't be long." Back in the classroom, the ruler was nowhere in sight. Tanya asked Mrs Smith. "Has anyone seen a ruler with a . . . what? Oh . . . a tiger on it?" Mrs Smith asked the class. "Isaac was using one like that," said Paula, "before break." Isaac looked flustered. "Yes, but I put it back." he said. "I remember, because I picked up my dinner money and then I . . ." He stopped. "Oh no . . . I've left my dinner money outside . . . I took it out but I haven't got a pocket, and I put it down . . !" He ran out of the room as the teacher was saying, "Well, you'd better go and fetch it . . ."

Tanya was horrified. How could she say that she had the money? Was it already too late to say so? She hadn't really meant to keep it, after all . . . had she? Would they believe her? But if Isaac had taken her ruler, it was fair that she kept the money, wasn't it? But what if she kept quiet and then Sam told everyone she had picked it up?

Isaac came back, nearly in tears. The money was gone. He would have to borrow enough to pay for his lunch, and somehow his Mum would have to find an extra pound tomorrow.

Jo thought of the ruler in her pencil case. She would throw it in the bushes on the way home. She couldn't use it in class now, because everyone would know it was Tanya's. And her Mum would ask where it had come from if she took it home.

"Tanya, what is wrong?" asked Mrs Smith.

Taking turns to speak and listen

Read these instructions aloud.

I am going to ask one person a question about the story. We will all listen to their ideas. I will ask why they think what they tell us, and we will all listen to their reasons.

Then that person will ask the next person, until we have all said what we think, and why we think it.

Next we can spend as long as we like talking together to decide on an answer to the question. We must try to agree on an answer. I am going to put a tick in these boxes to show that everyone had a turn at talking and listening at the start of our discussion. In this activity we must:
- ▲ take turns to talk and listen;
- ▲ make sure everybody has a chance to say something;
- ▲ try to agree on a group answer to the question.

Right? Let's start with Question 1 . . .

Questions to discuss:	Person 1	Person 2	Person 3	Person 4
What choices does Tanya have/what should she do?				
What choices does Jo have?				
Is stealing money worse than stealing a ruler?				
Is it wrong to steal – why?				

Reasoning with ground rules

Resources
Worksheets 5A: Visitors to the dogs' home and *5B: Dogs in the dogs' home*.

Aims
To apply all the ground rules for talk to reasoning problems. To ask relevant questions.

Introduction
Explain the aims of the lesson to the children. Ask the children to remember their ground rules for talk (which should be displayed on the wall of the classroom).

Introduce the activity by explaining that there are six stray dogs in the dogs' home. The staff of the dogs' home have made a list of them, describing their size, age, likes, dislikes and so on. (Provide *Worksheet 5B: Dogs in the dogs' home*, if you wish to explain this more fully.)

The dogs are available for adoption. On this particular day, five sets of people arrive at the dogs' home to look for a dog they can adopt and take home. We have some information about what sort of home they can give a stray dog. (Provide *Worksheet 5A: Visitors to the dogs' home*, for further explanation.)

The task for the groups is to think about the dogs and the people, and to talk together to make decisions about which owners would suit which dog. For example, Jack the bloodhound is very big and that is a good reason for deciding that he would not suit Mrs Jenkins, who has a small home.

The groups should be aware that they are practising using the ground rules, and that their discussion is the most important outcome of the lesson. They must concentrate on:

▲ asking for and giving reasons for suggestions;
▲ making sure everyone is heard;
▲ considering all ideas before coming to a group decision.

The dog left over at the end of the day will unfortunately have to be 'put down'! This makes rational debate particularly crucial.

(But for a reprieve, see follow-up work.)

Group work
Use the information to make decisions about which dog best matches which owner. (The sheets can be cut up if this helps: however, scissors may be a distraction from contributing to successful group talk.)

Plenary
Each group should give an example of which dog they have matched with which person, and support their decision with reasons. Ask the groups to say whether they found they could use the ground rules. Were the lesson aims achieved?

Follow up-work
▲ Dogs and owners could be stuck next to one another on a new sheet. Tell the groups that the 'condemned' dog may be rescued if they can talk together and decide on an ideal home/owners for the dog to go to. Set a time limit of five or ten minutes for this discussion. The group then explains their ideas and reasons to the class. A decision to reprieve the dog (or not!) is then made.

▲ Lesson 5A is optional, and can be used to extend the skills introduced in Lesson 5.

Visitors to the dogs' home

The Westons
Mr John Weston and Mrs Sue Weston, Tim, aged 10 and Lisa, aged 8. They have a house in a quiet street. Everybody goes out to work or school, but they are all home at weekends. The house has a large garden and there is a park 5 minutes away.

Mrs Jenkins
Mrs Sally Jenkins, who is aged 75, lives alone. Her son visits with her two grandchildren, Paul aged 3 and Sarah aged 1. She would love a dog for company. She lives in a small home with a very tiny back garden.

The Green Family
Mr Henry Green and Mrs Angela Green and Clara, aged 7. Clara has her own pony and two cats, she now she wants a dog. Angela is not very keen on dogs. They have a big house in the countryside, which has large garden and is surrounded by fields. They have a Land Rover and enjoy being out-of-doors.

The Carters
Mr Carter has two children, Sarah aged 16 and Mark aged 14. They live in a small house in town, with a park nearby. The children love dogs; Sarah wants to be a vet. Mr Carter would like a guard dog.

Miss Young
Miss Pamela Young, aged 30, has a ground floor flat. She works at home on most days. Her hobby is walking and she would like a dog to take with her. She sometimes has her nephew Russell, aged 8, to stay. She does not have a garden.

Dogs in the dogs' home

	Fifi	Jack
Name:	Fifi	Jack
Breed:	French poodle	Bloodhound cross
Male or female:	female	male
Age:	5 years	4 years
Size:	medium	large
Eats:	chicken and ham	large amounts
Guard dog:	no	yes
Likes:	children and other dogs	to sit by the fire
Dislikes:	rain and the vet	cats

	Cassie	Jess
Name:	Cassie	Jess
Breed:	Beagle	unknown
Male or female:	female	female
Age:	10 years	3 years
Size:	small	medium
Eats:	milk and biscuits	'Bonio' and dog food
Guard dog:	no	yes
Likes:	to be patted	people and playing
Dislikes:	running and snow	having to stay in

	Scooter	Gnasher
Name:	Scooter	Gnasher
Breed:	unknown	unknown
Male or female:	male	male
Age:	6 months	5 years
Size:	small	small
Eats:	shoes and 'Pedigree chum'	sausages
Guard dog:	no	yes
Likes:	going out to play	being naughty
Dislikes:	doing as he's told	softies and baths

Rainforest photographer

Resources
Sheets of 1cm-squared paper, pencils, rubbers, rulers, coloured crayons/felt tips.

Aims
This is an optional lesson, providing children with practice in using all the ground rules to reach decisions and accept joint responsibility. The lesson includes an element of mathematical problem-solving.

Introduction
This activity is a modified version of 'Battleships', in which children are paired to work with another pair (in groups of four). However, instead of sinking boats, the idea is to collect 'photographs' of a variety of animals within a given time. While there is a large degree of chance, problem-solving and reasoning skills are also necessary, in guessing which square the animal is in.

Group work
Children are paired. Each pair draws two grids on squared paper. The grids have the letters A to O along the base, and the numbers 1 to 15 up the left-hand side.

To prepare for play, each pair must first position their own animals on one grid. They must decide together which squares to use, and colour in their animals, using the following information:

One giant anteater	8 squares
Two jaguars	5 squares each
Three nine-banded armadillos	4 squares each
Four golden lion tamarinds	4 squares each
Five scarlet macaws	2 squares each
Six tree frogs	1 square

The animals must be separated by empty boxes, but can meet diagonally. The groups of boxes that make up an animal must join along their edges, not diagonally. This completed grid must be kept hidden.

The idea is that the group members are photographers, and their aim is to 'photograph' all the other team's animals, by guessing which square they are in. Each pair starts with both a blank grid, and their own completed grid. Toss a coin to decide which pair starts. The pair that starts must decide together, and choose a square using conventional grid referencing, e.g. square G8. The opposing team have to reveal what is in that square (either a blank, or the name of the animal).

Every time the players guess a blank square, the opposing team must provide them with information about the whereabouts of one of their hidden animals. This is done by starting at the blank square, and counting how many squares away (counting up/down/across, but not diagonally) the nearest animal is. The team may provide this information – but must not say in which direction the hidden animal is to be found.

	X			**Z**
		Guess		
Y				

In this example, if X, Y and Z are animals, the team's response would be: blank (the nearest animal is 3 boxes away). The aim is to 'photograph' all of the opponent's animals within the time limit.

Plenary
Check how many animals have been photographed. Ask if the class can suggest variations on the rules of the game. Question the groups about the strategies that they used in order to find the animals. Restate the lesson aims and discuss whether children feel that these have been achieved.

Follow up work
▲ Suggest variations on this game, e.g. Jungle safari using African animals; Sea-life food chain; Bird life; British wildlife; Space game (in which the items to be located are planets or constellations).
▲ Ask the class to devise their own versions.
▲ Children could also prepare grids to use with someone at home.

Section B
Talking, thinking and learning

Teachers' notes

The lessons in this section build on the skills and understanding developed in Section A. In Section B, children apply the ground rules for thinking to problem-solving and collaborative learning in different curriculum areas. It will be assumed that shared ground rules have been established in the class, so it is important to complete all of the Section A lessons first.

The ground rules are used throughout this section, but each lesson also highlights specific ground rules and aspects of thinking together. These will be explained in the lesson aims. A brief outline of each lesson is included along with the aims at the start of each lesson plan. As with the lessons in Section A, there are worksheets and suggestions for adapting or extending the activities. A brief outline of each lesson follows:

Lesson 6: Persuasion This provides three contexts in which children are required to use persuasive reasoning. First, the children practise using persuasive vocabulary in their speech, and are then asked to write a persuasive letter. Finally, a short drama activity allows the groups to share their understanding of the powers of persuasion.

Lesson 7: Kate's choice Children practise reasoning together in the area of citizenship, with a computer programme providing a context and prompt for reaching joint decisions. This lesson provides a template for using computers to encourage and support thinking together.

Lesson 8: Who pays? This builds on Lesson 7 to give children further opportunities to apply the ground rules, in trying to resolve a moral dilemma. A short story entitled 'Who pays?' is used to encourage children to make joint decisions and present their ideas as a group.

Lesson 9: Water voles The board game focuses on the plight of one of Britain's most endangered species, in order to encourage children's critical questioning and reasoning. Groups make joint decisions and present their ideas together.

Lesson 10: Town plan Children are asked to design a new town and must collect and share information with their group. This develops their ability to provide clear instructions, act upon them, and make joint decisions.

Lesson 11: A fair test   Using the context of a science investigation into materials, the children talk together to define a hypothesis and plan a 'fair test'. The groups are required to make joint decisions and present their agreed ideas.

Lesson 12: Non-fiction   Children use the ground rules for talk to discuss a non-fiction text. Whole-class work provides a structure for this activity, in which groups work collaboratively on reading for meaning.

Lesson 13: Looking into poems   Children study three poems together in this lesson, which provides opportunities for critical thinking. Individuals are required to justify their opinions with reasons.

Lesson 14: Staying friends   This lesson offers an additional citizenship context for practising the ground rules for talk. A short story provides the basis for discussion about which choices are available and why.

Lesson 15: Strategy   This lesson is another variation on the game of Battleships. It aims to encourage collaboration in pairs, with children accepting responsibility for joint decisions.

Lesson 16: Making a meaning web   Using ICT, co-operation between children, both face-to-face and at a distance, is established. The activities enable children to share relevant information, and to create resources together by communicating their ideas effectively. Children are encouraged to use the computer as a communication tool.

Persuasion

Resources
Worksheets 6A: Persuasive phrases and *6B: Making a letter more persuasive*.

Aims
To help children understand how language is used to persuade others. To teach the skills of persuasive talking and writing.

Introduction
Explain the aims for Lesson 6 to the children, and check that they understand the meaning of 'persuasion'. Briefly discuss some situations in which persuasion might be used, pointing out links between argument and agreement. Provide each group with a copy of *Worksheet 6A: Persuasive phrases*. Ask individuals to choose a phrase and use it in a sentence (spoken aloud). It might be necessary to provide a context for the persuasion, e.g. to be taken swimming/ shopping/ for a pizza/ to a football match, etc.

Group work

1. *Letter-writing*
Provide *Worksheet 6B: Making a letter more persuasive*. Ask the groups to talk together to rewrite the letter and make it more persuasive. They could use some of the words and phrases from the previous activity.

2. *Role-play*
Each group makes up a short scene in which one of them is a parent, and the others are children. The group then chooses to act out one of these scenarios, in which the child wishes to:

▲ go to the disco;
▲ stay up late to watch TV;
▲ be given more pocket money;
▲ have a friend to stay;
▲ have chips for tea;
▲ be allowed to have a pet.

The groups must be prepared to present their two-minute scene to the class.

Plenary

Groups present their 'Persuasion' scene to the class. The class discuss the effectiveness of the arguments, and vote on what the parent decides. Restate the lesson aims and discuss whether they have been achieved.

Follow up-work

▲ Children might be asked to discuss the ways that adults respond to persuasion. Discuss why adults might often end a discussion with phrases such as "because I say so!" or "when you get to my age . . .". Do children realise how much responsibility the adults have?

▲ Children could collect phrases or sayings about talk for illustration and display. Are they always true? These could be proverbs, or commonly-used phrases, such as: Actions speak louder than words... Don't do as I do, do as I say... Least said, soonest mended... He is all talk...

▲ Children could look at some of Aesop's fables, which deal with the phenomenon of persuasive talkers, or talkers who brag, tell lies, or attempt to mislead. The moral purpose of the story may be obvious, but it is useful to consider the talk strategies employed by the characters.

Persuasive phrases

As a result . . .

These are the facts . . .

Because . . .

Do you think that . . ?

But . . .

On the other hand . . .

Finally . . .

In my opinion . . .

I would like you to consider . . .

Perhaps we could discuss . . ?

In view of . . .

Eventually . . .

Instead . . .

However . . .

Perhaps . . .

To resolve this matter . . .

Please . . .

Next time . . .

I'd be glad if you'd think about . . .

So . . .

My reason is . . .

Because . . .

To begin with . . .

Against that, it could be said . . .

To look at it in another way . . .

The reason is . . .

Yet . . .

I can understand that . . .

To sort this out we could . . .

Maybe this time . . .

The best thing, I think, is to . . .

We could decide together . . .

Making a letter more persuasive

Name _____
Address _____
_____
_____

Dear (Gran/ Aunty/ Uncle/ Grandad),
Thank you for offering to take me to the museum for my birthday, but I don't want to go. Do we have to go? It's not fair - I don't even like museums. They are boring and full of old stuff. I want to go to the cinema. I need to see a film. I've got see [_____].

I will bring my friend along with me. I want to have popcorn and I am going to get a choc-ice too. And not only that, it had better be the 9 'o' clock show. Only little kids go early. You'd better take me to the cinema. Otherwise I will just be fed up and I will yawn a lot. If you don't like the cinema it is bad luck. You are just paying the money. It's my birthday and I can do what I like.

Best wishes,
From

[_____]

Kate's choice

Resources
'Kate's choice' software on the *Thinking Together* website. (This can be copied, and will run just by clicking on the icon.)
Worksheet 7: Argument frame.

Aims
To apply all the ground rules to reasoning about social and moral issues. To use a computer programme as a stimulus for thinking together. To deepen understanding of two citizenship issues (personal morality and the consequences of theft).

Introduction
Explain the aims of the lesson, stressing that the way the group talks together is an important focus. Raise and discuss the issue of keeping promises, asking the question: 'Is it ever right to break a promise?' Raise and discuss the issue of stealing from shops.

Group work
Option A: If there are enough computers for all talk groups.
Ask the children to work through 'Kate's choice' in their talk groups. Remind them of the ground rules for talk. Make sure that they have an agreed strategy for using the keyboard and mouse. Point out that the aim of the lesson is to do with talking and thinking, so it is not important who uses the mouse/keyboard. Despite this, it may be an idea to swap positions after about ten minutes. The software will normally take about 15 minutes to work through. If they finish quickly, ask them to try it again, taking a different route, and remind them to discuss the task together.

Option B: If there are fewer computers than groups.
Give the whole-class introduction to the activity, and then arrange for some of the children to work on 'Kate's choice' software in their groups while the other children are working on other group activities. When the whole class has had the opportunity to work on a computer, return to the plenary session.

Kate's choice

Kate has a friend called Robert, and Robert has a secret. He tells Kate the secret, on condition that she promises not to tell anyone else. It is his mother's birthday, and he has stolen a box of chocolates from a shop, to give to her. He decided to do this partly because his mother was ill. Kate has to decide whether to keep her promise, or whether to tell, and if so, who she should tell. The children have to talk over the issues raised, as Kate is put under pressure by various people. What choices are there for both Kate and Robert?

Plenary

Ask the children about their decision. Should Kate tell her parents straight away? Should she keep her promise and take the blame? Did they decide that Robert should be punished? What were their reasons? Remind them of the shopkeeper's perspective. Finally, ask the children to evaluate the quality of their discussion.

Follow up-work

Use Kate's choice as a stimulus for written argument either in the talk groups or for individuals using the 'argument frame' provided on *Worksheet 7*. An electronic version of the frame can be found on the *Thinking Together* website.

Other lessons

Using ICT

The plan for Lesson 7 can be adapted and used with other software. It represents an effective way of using software as a support for discussion. The aim of group discussion needs to be made explicit in the lesson aims, and the whole class session is crucial to ensure that children feel that they have achieved these aims. Through this process, they become aware that their talk together at the computer is an important contribution to their learning. Successful learning is more likely to be achieved where the children do not rush through the programme, or argue about who controls the mouse or keyboard.

Choosing software to encourage talk
Not all software is good for supporting thinking together.
Sometimes the best software is the simplest. You can use this chart
to analyse the potential of software for encouraging exploratory
talk. Consider the software that you have used, or seen in use with
children in the classroom, and tick the relevant boxes.

Questions	Yes	Partly	No
Is information which is useful for rational decision-making displayed on the screen?			
Are children offered choices that engage them in a continuing story or investigation?			
Are problems sufficiently complex?			
Do choices have important consequences?			
Are there multiple-choice options to encourage responses?			
Does the programme encourage collaborative activity?			

Ticks in the 'yes' column indicate that the software design
encourages and sustains discussion.

The Kate's choice software has been developed specifically to
promote learning through thinking together and is
complemented by the citizenship education pack *You, Me, Us*
produced by the Citizenship Foundation, 63 Charterhouse
Street, London EC1M 6HJ. The pack contains suggestions for
following up the moral issues raised in Kate's choice.
(See also Lesson 15)

Argument frame

Kate's choice by _____

> I/We decided that Kate should:

> I/We decided this because:

> Other people might think this the wrong decision because:

> However:

> When Robert admitted to stealing the chocolates, I/we decided that Robert should:

> I/We decided this because:

Who pays?

Resources
Worksheets 8A: Who pays? (a short story), *8B: Discussion format* and *8C: Drama cards* (to be photocopied and mounted separately on card).

Aims
To apply the ground rules to reaching joint decisions about social and moral dilemmas. To use discussion to increase children's awareness of the victims of crime.

Introduction
Explain the aims of the lesson to the children and ask children to remind each other of their ground rules for talk. Read, or ask a child to read, the short story on *Worksheet 8A*.

Remind the children that it is fine to disagree with another person's ideas, as long as you do so calmly and politely, and can provide a reason for disagreeing. It is useful to stress that disagreeing with someone need not mean that you dislike that person.

Group work
Using *Worksheet 8B*, ask the groups of children to discuss the issues raised by the questions. Groups could then try the following activities:

1. Ask the groups to contribute to a whole class discussion about the issues raised by the story.
2. Ask each group to make up a three-minute theatre play. The groups are given a subject for their play (see *Worksheet 8C*).

Ask the children to read the drama cards together and decide how to present the story to the class. Only the simplest of props will be allowed, and the script should not be written down.

Plenary
Each group presents its play to the rest of the class as audience. Pupils then check that the lesson aims have been fulfilled.

Follow-up work

▲ Video or tape-record the children's plays.

▲ Use the plays as a basis for a whole class discussion of the issues raised.

▲ Ask the children to write their own stories using the characters of Sam, Tanya, Henry, and any more they care to imagine. The story should tackle a 'problematic' issue, e.g. friendships; similarities and differences between people; telling the truth; respect; anger; appearances; rights and responsibilities, etc. Stories do not have to resolve issues or have happy endings, but should highlight potential problems caused by people's behaviour.

Other lessons

Choose another story, which contains a moral dilemma and approach it in the same way. *Worksheet 8B* could be adapted for this purpose. Using this structure, the children could progress to independently organising their own discussions, using the ground rules for talk.

Who pays? A short story

The Mini Market was a little shop on the corner of Main Street and Clarence Road. Sam lived in Clarence Road, and often went to the shop before school to buy crisps or a drink for her packed lunch. Lots of other children went to the shop in the morning too. If the children had any pocket money, they would also go after school, to buy an ice cream or sweets. The shop was always full of children. Mr and Mrs Bell owned the shop. They kept it open very late in the evening, and it was open all weekend too. Sam didn't know how early they opened in the morning, but it was much earlier than she ever got up. Mr and Mrs Bell's son Henry was in Sam's class at school, and she knew that he often helped put things out on the shelves. It looked like fun.

Sam knocked on Tanya's door. "Ready?" They set off to walk to school. Tanya was happy because the Book Fair was opening in school at lunchtime. You could choose a book to buy, and she had enough money for the next book in her favourite animal series. "Are you going to buy a book, Sam?" she asked. "Oh, I'd forgotten it started today. Well, maybe tomorrow. Look – I've only got 30p for my crisps." "Salt and vinegar as usual, I suppose," said Tanya.

There were lots of people in the shop. There were three girls from Year 7, and two boys from Year 6. A man in a suit was buying a box of chocolates, and a lady with a small child in a push-chair was buying a newspaper. Mr Bell was serving behind the till. It seemed very crowded in the little shop. Everyone was pushing past each other and tripping over the newspapers and the push-chair. Suddenly the shop emptied and Sam went to pay for her crisps.

Mr Bell was looking worried and cross. "Look," he said to Sam and Tanya. "I'm fed up of you kids coming in here. I can't afford it any longer." They looked at one another in surprise. What did he mean? "Every morning and every afternoon this shop is full of kids," he said, waving his arms around. "Gangs . . . gangs of kids. And when you've gone, so have half of my boxes of sweets, and whole packets of biscuits, and . . . look! You can see now, four or five cans have gone, and no-one's paid for them."

They still couldn't think what to say. Mrs Bell arrived in the shop from the door at the back.

"They've done it again. Taken a load of cans, and goodness knows what else," he said to her. "We just can't afford it any longer." He turned to Sam and took her money. "You kids, just taking things like that . . . and then Henry wants money to buy a book at school. How am I supposed to find money for books if people carry on stealing from us?"

Mrs Bell sat down on the chair behind the counter. She looked very sad. "What are we going to do?" she said. "It's hopeless. Henry works so hard for us, when he'd really rather be out playing, and yet we can't even give him the money for a book!" Tanya was out of the door first. As Sam shut the door behind her, Tanya said, "Do you think they are poor, then? I always thought people who had shops were rich. They've got all that stuff, after all." "Yes, and he said it was stealing, but it's shoplifting, isn't it?" said Sam. "Stealing from a shop isn't the same as stealing from a person, I reckon. And they are always open. They must make lots of money." "I'm not so sure," said Tanya. "If people only buy packets of crisps or newspapers or milk, you know, fairly cheap things, they would have to sell an awful lot to make any money for themselves." "They made me feel as if it was my fault!" said Sam. "That's not fair."

They ran into the playground as the bell rang.

Who pays? A discussion format

Instructions
Read the following instructions aloud to the class:

> We are going to use the ground rules for talk to think together about the questions on this sheet. We will start by taking it in turns to say what we think and why, and I will put a tick in the boxes as that happens. Then we can discuss our ideas.
>
> Right? Let's start with Question 1...

Questions for discussion:	Writer:	1	2	3
Is 'shoplifting' the same as stealing?				
What is the same about it – what is different?				
Is shoplifting wrong – why?				
Would it be wrong for someone to 'shoplift' some food if they had no money and were very hungry?				
Which of the people in the shop was most likely to be a shoplifter?				
How can you tell?				
Sam thought it wasn't fair that Mr Bell was angry with her – do you agree?				
Does it matter more or less whether someone shoplifts from a small shop (like Mr and Mrs Bell's) or a big shop like Woolworth's?				
How should shoplifters be punished?				

Who pays? Drama cards

Scissors

Mr Smith watches as Luke goes into the stock cupboard. Luke comes out with empty hands, but Mr Smith can see the handles of a pair of scissors sticking out of his pocket. He thinks Luke has stolen them. Luke has not been caught stealing before. But a lot of things have gone missing from the classroom recently, and Mr Smith wants to make sure it stops.

What choices does Mr Smith have? What does he do? What does Luke say?

Brothers

Andy thinks that his older brother Paul has been stealing from the local shop. His friend Mark has told him that he saw Paul go along with a crowd of his friends and steal some sweets and drinks. He doesn't want to get Paul into trouble. But on the other hand, Andy doesn't want Paul to be a thief.

What choices does Andy have? What should he do? What happens?

Treasure

You and a friend are playing near some bushes. Hidden under a bush you find a wallet, carefully wrapped in a polythene bag. It has obviously been hidden there for some reason. Inside the wallet there is £15.00 in cash and a photograph, but no name.

What choices do you have? What do you do? What happens?

Supermarket

You are out shopping in the supermarket. You notice that an elderly lady puts a tin of baked beans into her shopping bag, not into the trolley.

What choices do you have? What do you do? What happens?

Shopkeeper

Your friend has been caught stealing sweets from the shop. You have to go to the shop to get milk for your family. The shopkeeper follows you all round the shop. You ask why and he says he doesn't trust you, and asks you to leave.

Is this fair? What happens?

Ice-lollies

You and your sister go out to play. It is a hot day. You both get very thirsty but you are some way from home. Your sister tells you to wait outside the shop while she goes in to get some ice-lollies. You know that she doesn't have any money.

What do you say to her? What do you both do? What happens?

Window-sill

You and your friend are playing outside at break-time. You find 50p on the window-sill outside one of the classrooms. Your friend picks it up and says she will give it to the teacher. However, after school she offers you a sweet that she has just bought. You realise that she kept the money.

What do you say? What does she do? What happens?

Bully

You meet the school bully outside the shop. He says he wants a Mars Bar, and demands that you give him some money. You don't have any money. He says that unless you go in and steal him a lolly, he will wait for you and beat you up on the way home.

Should you do as he says? What choices do you have? What happens?

Dares

You go out to play with your friends and you all decide to play 'dares'. The group dares someone to go into the shop and steal some crisps. One of your friends manages to do it. You all share the crisps. Then it's your turn. Your friends dare you to go and get some Smarties.

What choices do you have? What happens?

Apples

Your neighbour has an apple tree full of apples. She tells you that she is going to give them to your school for the Harvest Festival. But, that night, lots of the apples are stolen. Next day your friend offers you a bag of apples – which have obviously come from the tree.

What choices do you have? What happens?

Watch

After PE, Tom's watch goes missing. Everyone looks but it is nowhere to be found. Tom is afraid his parents will be angry. That afternoon, you go round to play at your friend's house, and you suddenly notice Tom's watch in the friend's bedroom.

What do you say? What does your friend say? What happens?

Rewards

It is near the end of term, and the teacher has brought in a bag of sweets to give to people who have earned a reward. At break, you have to go back to the classroom to collect something, and you notice that the bag is open on the desk. You would love a sweet and think to yourself that it would be all right if you took one for your friend too. Then you think again.

What do you decide to do? Why? What would someone else do?

Water voles

Resources

The following resources are for the 'Water vole' board game: *Teacher information sheet 9A: About the water vole. Teacher information sheet 9B: How to make the water vole board game. Sheet 9A: Water vole game people information. Sheet 9B: Water vole game labels. Sheet 9C: Water vole game chance cards. Sheet 9D: Water vole game rules. Sheet 9E: 'Water vole year' game-board. Sheet 9F: Set of water vole colony cards.*

Before the lesson, please follow the instructions on *Teacher information sheet 9B.*

Aims

To encourage children's critical questioning and reasoning. To give children more practice in making joint decisions and presenting ideas as a group. To deepen awareness of issues in ecology.

Introduction

Explain the aims of the lesson and ensure that the children recall the importance of using the ground rules for talk in their discussions. Use *Teacher information sheet 9A* to give a brief description of the plight of water voles as they move towards extinction in England. Then explain the object and rules for the board game, as follows:

Rules
The object of the game is to go through a year along the river, finding out what factors affect the water vole colonies. Colonies can be lost or gained. Players shake a dice and move along the 'river'. If they land on a chance square, they take a card. Some of the cards direct the players to listen to the opinions of various people who wish to alter the riverbank. One player should read out each opinion.

The group then discusses the opinions (using their ground rules for talk) and decides whether or not to approve the change proposed. When all players have landed on the last square, the group should assess the river to see how many water vole colonies have survived.

Group work

Ask the children to work through the board game in their talk groups.

Plenary

Compare results of the board game, as a class. Change groups – new groups need not be the usual talk groups – and start again with the game. The ground rules for talk should still apply. To make things more difficult (or realistic) groups could start from the position they were in at the end of the previous 'year'. Finally, ask the children to evaluate the quality of their discussions.

Follow-up work

Find out more about water voles from as many sources as possible – books, CD-ROMs, conservation groups, the Internet.

Other lessons

Look at a different conservation issue involving loss of species through habitat destruction, e.g.

▲ mahogany trees in the Amazon rain forest;
▲ mountain gorillas in Rwanda;
▲ whales in the waters around Japan;
▲ cod in the North Atlantic;
▲ polar bears in the Arctic circle;
▲ kiwi in New Zealand;
▲ platypus in Australia;
▲ tigers in Siberia;
▲ snow leopards in Tibet.

Consider the factors that cause habitat destruction in terms of the lives of the local people. What issues arise? What are the similarities with the problems for water voles?

About the water vole

The water vole was immortalised as 'Ratty' by Kenneth Grahame in *The Wind in the Willows*, published in 1908. Water voles have found it increasingly difficult to survive as their riverside environment changed throughout the last century. They are now the most endangered British mammals. The board game demonstrates some of the uses people have found for river banks, and asks the children to discuss their opinions on whether the needs of water voles or the requirements of people should be given priority.

Water voles prefer slow-moving water and river banks which are rich in vegetation. They excavate burrows in the banks and line them with shredded rushes or reeds. They are herbivorous, feeding on grasses, rushes and sedges from the banks, and fruits and roots in autumn and winter. Water voles live in colonies along the banks and breeding begins in March or April. In April or May two to six young are born. At first they are helpless: blind, hairless and toothless – but at ten days old they have become miniature versions of the adults, and at 28 days they are weaned.

The water vole has a wide range of traditional predators including foxes, otters, stoats, weasels, rats, owls, herons, raptors and large fish. Domestic cats can also cause extinction of local colonies. A new problem is the rising number of American mink, either escaped, or released from fur farms. Studies have shown that water vole populations within the territories of breeding female mink can be decimated within a year. Loss of habitat is another cause of population reduction. Some estimates put the population of water voles as low as 200,000 (that is 3,000 colonies). These numbers may sound large but the water vole is at the bottom of the food chain: there are, for example, 37 million rabbits in Britain, 31 million moles, and 75 million field voles. The water vole used to be common, but is now scarce.

Further information on water voles
Water Voles, Rob Strachan: Whittet Books Ltd. 18, Anley Rd, London W14 OBY. Water Vole Steering Group: Environment Agency, Kings Meadow House, Kings Meadow Rd, Reading RG1 8DQ. The British Waterways Environmental and Scientific Services: Llanthony Warehouse, Gloucester Docks, Gloucester GL1 2BJ. BBONT Wildlife Trust Ltd: 1 Armstrong Rd, Littlemore, Oxford, OX4 4XT.

How to make the water vole board game

1. Each group should have a *water vole year game-board* (*Sheet 9E*) preferably A3 size, which they can colour and laminate, if necessary.

2. Each group should have a copy of the *people information sheet* (*9A*). This should be cut up (so that there are 9 separate cards) and glued on to card, with the appropriate label (from sheet 9B) stuck on to the reverse side of the card. These are then placed face down next to the board.

3. The chance cards (9C) are cut up, glued on to card, and placed face down on the board.

4. The water vole colonies (on sheet 9F) should also be backed with card. Place eight of the colony cards on the board, and the rest beside the board.

5. Each child has a counter, to be placed at the beginning.

6. Before starting, the groups should read the instructions and check that they understand how to play the game. They should also know what the aims of the game are. They should not read through the people information or chance cards.

Water vole game: people information

Animal rights activist
 I love animals. I think they have the right to be wild and free. 'Activist' means I take action – and I take action to help animals. Near here there is a mink farm. Mink are little furry creatures, like cats, but fiercer, and they can swim. They are from America. The mink farmer keeps them in tiny metal cages. Then when they are big enough, he kills them and skins them, and sells their fur to make coats. It is very cruel. It shouldn't be allowed. The mink are suffering. I am going to go and let them all out of their cages, so that they can be free. That will teach the mink farmer a lesson. I know that mink eat lots of water voles. But the water voles can look after themselves. They can breed to replace the ones that get eaten. It is more important to let those poor creatures out of their cages than it is to worry about a few water voles. There are plenty more of them. Mink eat rats too, so they are useful really. Helping water voles survive isn't my problem at the moment – think of the mink.

I am going to free as many mink as I can – why not?

Fisherman
I love animals. I love fish, and that's why I like to catch them. I don't think water voles matter very much except that they are good food for the pike. I want to be able to sit nearer the water, so I want the edge of the bank flattened. The water voles have dug out the bank and made it crumbly, so I think we should get it repaired, and have proper concrete platforms put along here; then people can use it again. My hobby costs me a lot of money. I pay for this river to be kept clean and tidy so that I can fish in it. Because I pay money, I am good for the environment – the River Authority makes sure the water pollution levels stay low, so that there are always fish. I have the right to a good place to fish. The water voles can go and live somewhere else.

I am going to make sure that there are concrete platforms put along the bank – why not?

Water vole game: people information

Farmer

I love animals. I know all about them, which most people don't. I also know that people need to eat, and I have to grow their food. It doesn't come from nowhere to the supermarket, you know! Things have been difficult recently, with the bad weather. Now I am going to plough up the field next to the river, because I have to. When I do this, I will get some money from the government, so I will be able to buy a new tractor and grow more food. I will be able to get some good seed for next year and to grow some sugar beet in the field. It will grow well there. There is plenty more river for water voles. It is only one field, or maybe two, and I need the money. Look – if I grow the sugar beet it can be turned into sugar for sweets – you wouldn't like to go without those, would you? Where are you going to get food from, if I don't grow it?

I am going to plough up the field by the river – why not?

Dog owner

I love animals. I've got one – this dog. You might call those things water voles, but they look like rats to me. I get my dog to chase them. It's fun, and doesn't do any harm. It doesn't hurt them you know. They don't feel things like we do. And they are vermin; they are just like rats and can spread disease. Me and my dog are doing you a favour by catching a few. Anyway my dog is an animal too and he needs the exercise. It's good for a dog to run after other things. It's only natural. I've always trained my dogs to go after rats and rabbits. Otherwise the countryside would be over-run by them, like in Australia. There would be too many and the grass would die. I can do what I like anyway.

I am going to get my dog to chase them – why not?

Water vole game: people information

Land developer

I love animals. My job is to build homes for people and their pets. I have to find empty places to build new homes. People have to live in houses, and there aren't enough of them. How would you like it if you were homeless? I turn empty spaces into wonderful new housing estates, with homes for people who need them. I don't think a few holes for water voles should stand in the way of homeless people getting somewhere to live, do you? And by the river here, the houses will have a lovely view. We can tidy up the bank and have a nice path, so people can walk without getting muddy. The water voles really ought to be living somewhere else, I think. They could keep them safe in a zoo, or take them to another river. People need houses. They don't need water voles.

I am going to build a housing estate – why not?

Factory owner

I love animals. I have some terrific guard dogs at my factory. My factory is just up the river from here. It has been there a long time. We take water from the river to cool the machinery, then put it back in. I have spent a lot of money on cutting down the pollution we put into the water. We are doing our best. There might be the odd leak of poisonous chemicals sometimes, but it is always an accident. If it kills off the fish and water voles, it can't be helped. They always come back, don't they? The thing is, I employ 250 people. I pay their wages, so they can feed their kids and get them new trainers, trips to the cinema, birthday presents and parties. I can't help it if there are accidents at the factory sometimes. My machines are getting a bit old and I could spend more money on making sure they don't poison the river. But if I do, I will have to cut people's wages.

I am going to keep on using the river like I always have – why not?

Water vole game: people information

Boat owner

I love animals. My cat comes with me on the boat. It is a canal boat. We want to use this bit of river to link one canal with another. It just needs the sides straightening, really. It would only take a week or so with a JCB digger, and it would be done. Very neat and tidy. Then lots of boats could come up and down here. People like boat trips, and it helps stop cars polluting the air if people use boats. It is only a small stretch of river – there is plenty more for the water voles in other places. The boats will make money, so the River Authority can keep the water quality good, too. It will be very good for the river. Just think, you could go on a boat trip down here – wouldn't that be fun?

I am going to straighten out the banks of the river – why not?

Park keeper

I love animals. I have cages with rabbits in the park. The park is just along the river and we have swans and ducks and moorhens. We make sure that they are looked after. If we made the riverbank part of the park, we could have more swans and ducks and moorhens. We would need to tidy it up though. Those willow trees are leaning over the water in a way that is dangerous. What if one of them fell on someone? We could tidy up the bushes, so that there would be a better view. Then people could walk here more easily. If we had a park here, they would never be able to build houses on it. People could come here and play football, or ride bikes, or whatever they liked. There is plenty of wildlife out in the countryside. In town, we need to use the land for people.

I am going to get my strimmer and sort out that riverbank – why not?

Water vole game: people information

Most people

We love animals. We have pets and bird-tables. But water voles are like rats, and rats are dirty creatures that spread disease. We have never seen a water vole, so they can't be that important. You can live without water voles. It is more important to have good homes, plenty to eat, and good facilities like parks. Who says that water voles are endangered? It's probably not true. They are probably just saying it to get some money off us. It might be nice to have them in the river, but there are minks here now and they are just as interesting. Anyway if water voles are nearly extinct, it's too late to worry about it. There are probably millions of them in Norway or somewhere. It's the Amazon rainforest we should be worrying about. We have stopped buying mahogany from B&Q, so we are doing our bit. Did you say that there are practically no voles left here?

That's a shame, but I'm going to carry on doing nothing about it – why not?

Water vole game: labels

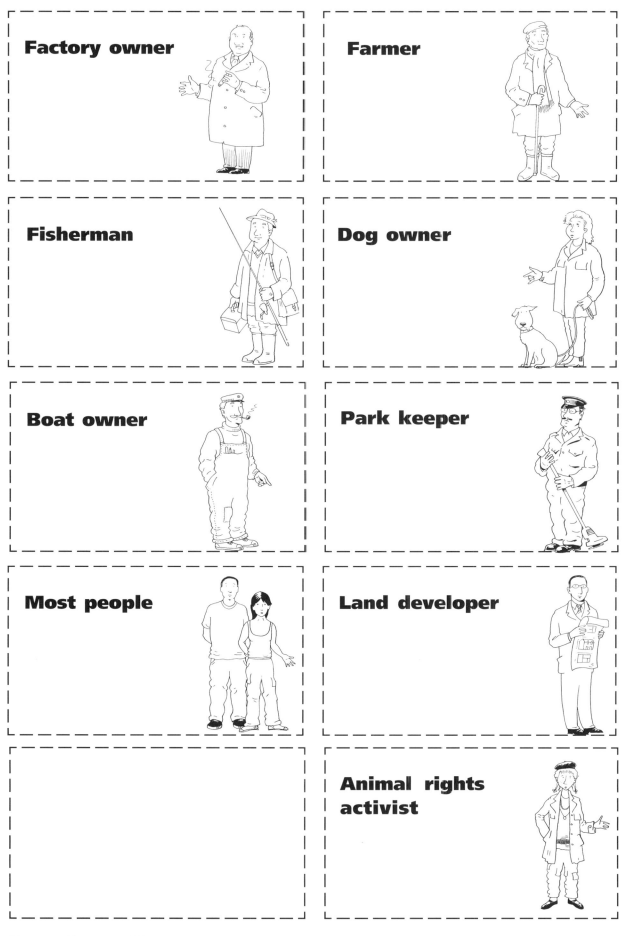

Factory owner

Farmer

Fisherman

Dog owner

Boat owner

Park keeper

Most people

Land developer

Animal rights activist

Water vole game: chance cards

School children measure water pollution: water vole family moves in!

FLOOD! Lose a water vole family.

School children do a water vole survey: water vole family moves in!

MINK! Eats a water vole family.

School children do a litter collection: water vole family moves in.

PIKE! Eats a water vole family.

School children write to the River Authority: water vole family moves in.

FOX! Eats a water vole family.

School children learn about water voles: water vole family moves in.

HERON! Eats a water vole family.

Water vole game: chance cards

WEASEL!
Eats a water vole family.

Let's hear what the
FISHERMAN has to say.

Let's hear what the
ANIMAL RIGHTS ACTIVIST
has to say.

Let's hear what the DOG
OWNER has to say.

Let's hear what the
FARMER has to say.

Let's hear what the
FACTORY OWNER has to
say.

Let's hear what the LAND
DEVELOPER has to say.

Let's hear what the BOAT
OWNER has to say.

Let's hear what the PARK
KEEPER has to say.

Let's hear what MOST
PEOPLE have to say.

Water vole game: rules

1. The game is for two to four players.

2. The aim of the game is to discuss some of the things that make it easier or harder for water voles to survive.

3. Set out the board as follows:

▲ put the chance cards on the 'chance cards' box;
▲ put the people information cards (face down) to one side;
▲ put one counter for each player at the beginning of the game;
▲ put eight water vole colony cards out along the riverbank.

4. Decide who goes first: shake the dice and move along the board. When you get to a chance square, take a card from the board and follow the instructions. (The group can decide who reads out the people information cards.)

Remember to talk about the ideas.

If the group decides to agree with the people information card, a water vole colony card is removed from the board. If the group disagrees with the people card, the colonies stay as they are.

5. When everyone has landed on 'end', count up the colony cards:

▲ more than eight colonies – the water voles will survive for another year;
▲ four to seven colonies – the water voles may survive, but will need good luck and help;
▲ less than four colonies – the water voles are dangerously close to vanishing from this river;
▲ less than two colonies – the water voles will become extinct here.

WATER VOLE YEAR

BEGIN
MARCH 21ST

SPRING

2

3

APRIL 21ST

5

MAY 21ST

CHANCE

SUMMER

JUNE 21ST

8

7

11

10

12

JULY 21ST

14

15

16

AUGUST 21ST

If you land on a ✳ square, take a chance and talk about it.

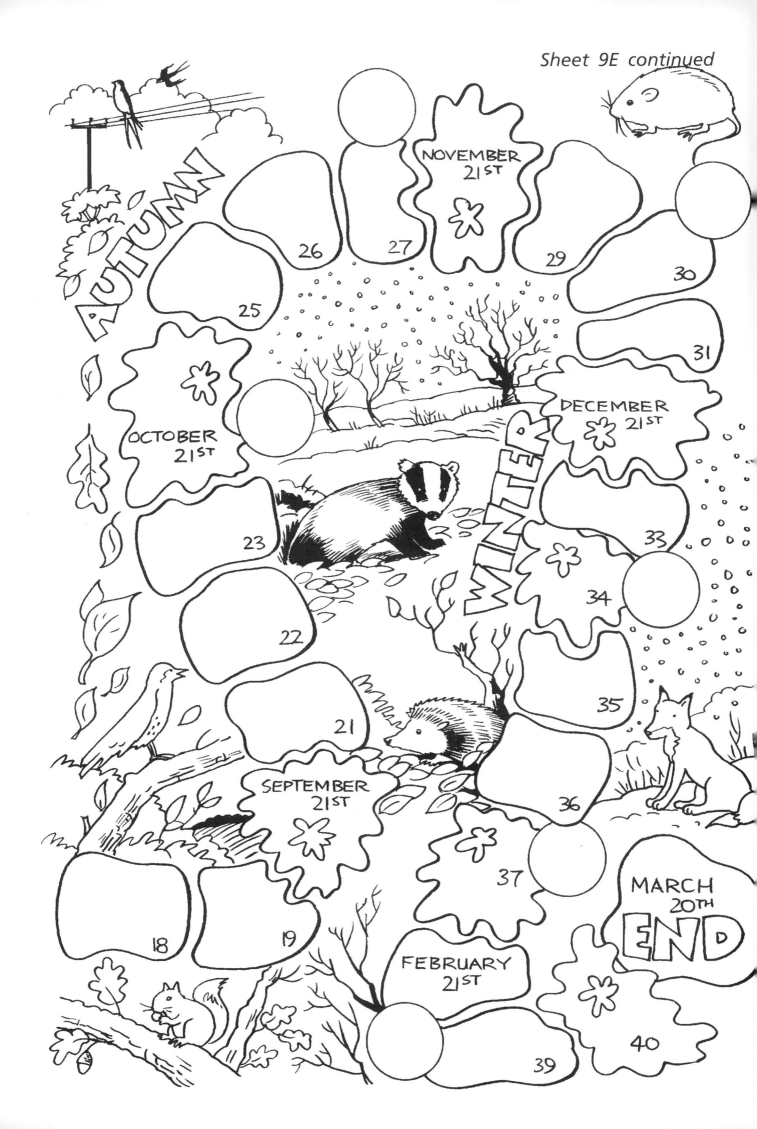

Water vole colony cards

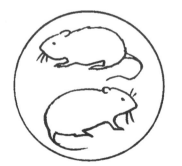

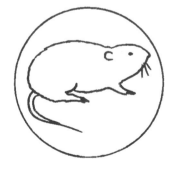

Town plan

Resources
Worksheets *10A: Town plan*, *10B: Facilities* and *10C: Information items*.

Aims
To develop children's ability to provide clear instructions and act upon them. To encourage joint decision-making using all the ground rules for talk. To promote awareness of planning and environmental issues.

Introduction
Explain the lesson aims and the town planning activity to the children, using the following information. The task for each group is to plan the best possible new town. To do this, each group should discuss how they could arrange the new facilities on the town plan. Some of the facilities are:

▲ swimming pool
▲ toilets
▲ petrol station
▲ school
▲ church
▲ factory

The group must consider and decide where they think each facility should be, in the town. Remind children to give reasons for ideas, and to try to come to a group decision.

Worksheet 10C: Information items, gives directions and reasons for the positioning of six of the facilities (those listed above). Cut up the sheet into separate items and give each talk group in the class one item (or two, if there are less than six groups.)

Group work
When a group requires information about one of these six facilities, one member should visit another group, who must read the information to them. The visitor is not allowed to read the information or write it down, but must listen and remember it to repeat to their own group. Each member of the group must carry out this task in turn, as the need arises.

Plenary

Set up a whole-class discussion about the position of facilities in the new town, giving reasons for their ideas. Ask children how easy or difficult it was to memorise and pass on the information received as visitors to another group. Ask children to talk together and decide on a name for the town. Can they think of anything they would add to the plan in order to improve the town? Check that the lesson aims have been fulfilled.

Follow-up work
▲ Display the town plans, with written reasons for the choice of layout.
▲ Try to think of reasons why your local town, village or city is laid out as it is.

Town plan

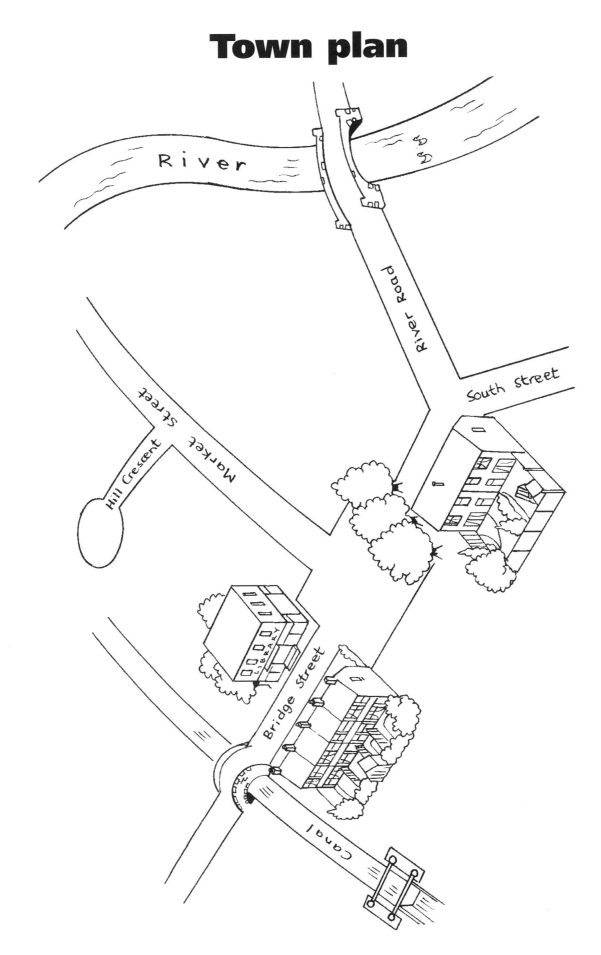

Facilities

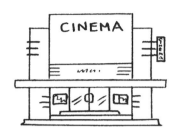

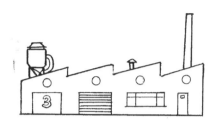

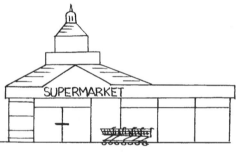

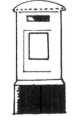

Information items

Swimming pool

The swimming pool must be near to the school, because the children need to go for lessons, and the school does not have a minibus. It should also be quite near the car park, because people don't like walking too far to their cars when they are tired.

Toilets

These must be near the park so that people can find them easily, when they are out. They must also be near the shops, for the same reason.

Petrol station

This must not be too near the houses, as it could be a fire risk.

School

This must not be too near the garage, as it could be a fire risk. It should also be away from the rubbish tip, because that would be bad for children's health.

Church

This must be near the centre of the town, so that it is within walking distance for people who want to go there.

Factory

This must not be near the houses or school, because it is noisy. It should be near the car park, so that people can park there to go to work.

A fair test

Resources

Worksheet 11: Science planning. Six or more 'kitchen cupboard' chemicals to display, e.g. white/cube/brown sugar; flour; custard powder; Andrews liver salts; cornflour; oatbran; ground rice; rock/table/dishwasher salt; nutmeg; corn oil; gravy granules; etc.

Aims

To give children practice in making joint decisions and presenting ideas as a group. To apply the ground rules to define a hypothesis and plan a 'fair test' for investigation.

Introduction

Explain the lesson aims, then show the children the different 'chemicals'. Make it clear that they might be edible in the kitchen, but in science lessons, all chemicals are regarded as poisonous and must not be put in or near the mouth. Check that the children understand what is meant by the words dissolve and solution. Ask them to explain these terms in their own words.

Then, describe the following science problem to the class:

Kitchen chemicals: an investigation about dissolving

It was raining and Isaac and Simon had nothing to do. They had to stay in. They decided they would act out being scientists, and turn the kitchen into a science laboratory. 'We need some chemicals to mix,' said Isaac. 'There are lots of things in the cupboard,' said Simon. 'Everything is a chemical really! We should do an experiment.' 'OK,' said Isaac, 'an investigation.' 'Let's find out which of these chemicals dissolves in water,' said Isaac, pouring sugar into a cup full of water. 'Hang on,' said Simon, 'if we really want to know, we have to do a fair test to find out.'

The group's task is to design a fair test investigation to find out which of the chemicals will dissolve in water.

Give each group a copy of *Worksheet 11* and stress the need to use the ground rules for talk, in this planning activity.

Group work
Using *Worksheet 11*, each group must write down their hypothesis stating which chemicals will dissolve and which will not, with reasons, and plan an investigation to test their hypothesis.

Plenary
Each group pairs up with another group and shows what they have decided to do. Then, in turns, each group should state and justify their hypothesis and make clear how they will ensure that they conduct a fair test. Members of the other group can ask questions about this. In a whole-class discussion, individuals should give an account of their group's ideas and hypothesis. Repeat the lesson aims and check that they have been fulfilled.

Follow-up work
▲ Let the groups carry out the investigation. Each group should decide on how best to display its results.
▲ Review the importance of the use of the ground rules in this work.
▲ Plan a similar investigation, e.g., to see if substances dissolve at different rates in warm water, or to decide which ice cube (of four differently-shaped ones) will melt fastest when dropped in water. This time, allow no conferring, discussion of ideas, or sharing of information. Once the plans are complete, organise a class discussion to decide which is the most effective way to plan an investigation, either in groups using the ground rules, or alone.

Other lessons
Worksheet 11 can be adapted to provide a document which will support discussion at the planning stage of any science investigation.

Talking about an investigation

1
Discuss the following: 1. What shall we actually do? 2. Can we draw a diagram to show this? 3. What equipment shall we use?

2
Discuss the following: To make it a fair test, what one thing will we change each time? What things will we make sure stay the same?

3
Discuss the following: How will we record our results?

4
Discuss the following: Before we do the investigation, we have to predict which chemicals will dissolve. (That is, we have to say what we think and give a reason for it.) This prediction is called a hypothesis. Can you complete the following?

Our hypothesis is that these chemicals will dissolve because:

_____

Our hypothesis is that these chemicals will not dissolve because:

_____

These are our group's ideas. Signed:

_____

Non-fiction

Resources
Worksheets 12A: 'Goose bumps', 12B: 'Friction' and *12C: 'Structure for group work'*. Dictionaries and thesaurus.

Aims
To encourage children to use the ground rules for talk to discuss a written text. To develop children's ability to read for meaning. To deepen understanding of friction as a scientific concept.

Introduction
Explain the aims of the lesson to the children and ask them to remember the ground rules for talk. Remind the children that their talk together is of paramount importance, and that in this lesson they will use their spoken language to improve their reading. Provide each group with a copy of *Worksheet 12A: 'Goose bumps'* or display the text on an overhead projector/ whiteboard. Ask fluent readers to read the text out loud to the class. Explain that the class is going to ask questions about the text to make sure that everyone really understands what it means. Check that the children understand what a 'paragraph' is. Guide the children towards deciding together on the following:

▲ any words that must be clarified by looking in a dictionary, or by talking to one another;
▲ three 'key words' for each paragraph;
▲ a summary of what each paragraph is about;
▲ two questions that each paragraph would answer;
▲ a new title for the text.

Group work
Using *Worksheet 12B*, the groups should talk together to establish meaning from the text, as in the whole-class work. *Worksheet 12C* will provide a structure for the group discussions.

Plenary
Ask groups to contribute their agreed ideas to a class discussion of the questions on *Worksheets 12B* and *12C*. Restate the lesson aims and check that these have been fulfilled.

Follow-up work
Ask each group to compile a pamphlet or poster on the topic of 'friction' using what they have learnt, as well as other sources.

Other lessons
This lesson plan, which helps children to make sense of information texts, can easily be adapted. *Worksheet 12C* can be used as a framework for looking at texts in any curriculum area.

'Goose bumps'

Why do I get goose bumps when I'm cold?

Goose bumps are trying to keep you warm! You belong to a group of animals called mammals. All mammals can feed their babies with milk. Mammals don't have feathers or scales – they have skin with hair or fur. Hair keeps you warm. It does this by trapping a warm layer of air next to the skin. When any furry mammal gets cold, its hair 'stands on end'. That makes the hair hold even more air, which keeps the warmth in.

You wear clothes to keep you warm. But your skin and hair still work like any other mammal. The hair you do have, even though there isn't much of it, can 'stand on end' to hold air and to help keep you warm. The 'bumps' of goose bumps are where you can see this happening, at the roots of the hair on your skin.

You get goose bumps when you are scared, too. This time your hair stands on end to make it stick out more, and make you look bigger and fiercer. Have you ever noticed that cats and dogs do this when they are scared? They get goose bumps too!

Friction

Isaac Newton was a famous scientist. He thought about the way things seemed to work in the world around him, and then tested his ideas to see if they were right. He was very interested in the way light works, in maths, and in the way things move. He tried to find out what makes things move, and what makes things stop. He found out that things started moving if there was a force pushing them, pulling them, or turning them round. Newton made a list of rules or laws, which describe the way things move in our Universe. Another word for movement is 'motion'. We call these rules 'Newton's Laws of Motion'.

This is one of Newton's Laws of Motion: Every moving thing in the universe carries on moving, just as it is, unless a force acts on it to stop it, or change its direction. This seems hard to understand. That is because we are used to seeing moving things slow down and stop all by themselves. We have all noticed that if we kick a ball along the ground it will soon slow down and stop moving. The ball started moving because it was kicked. A kick is a pushing force, and the force of the kick makes the ball move. But what stops it moving? It just seems to stop when it has run out of energy.

The ball stops because there is a force called friction. Friction is a force that acts to slow moving things down. Another word for friction is 'grip'. This is how we think friction works. Moving things slide or run over each other like the football rolls over the grass. While this is happening the surface (or outside) of the football touches the grass. The surface of the football is fairly smooth to touch, but if you could look at it under a microscope, you would see it is made of lots of little 'hills and valleys'. The surface of the grass is quite rough, even to touch. As these surfaces move over each other, the rough bits catch on each other, and slow down the movement.

If we slide a smooth stone over a frozen pond, t will move a long way before it stops. Both the surfaces are unusually smooth, so there is not much friction. If we try to clean a carpet by brushing it with a stiff brush, it is very hard work. There is a lot of friction between the two rough surfaces. We have to use a lot of energy to overcome the large force of friction, which we are creating by moving the brush over the carpet. (So that's why Mr. Hoover invented his carpet cleaner!)

Friction is useful. It helps us get a grip on the ground. We wear shoes with rough soles so that we don't slide about. We put gripping tyres on our cars so that they hold the (rough) surface of the road and make driving safe. But friction can also be a nuisance. Inside car engines, the surfaces of the metal parts move over each other, and create friction. If nothing was done about it, this friction force would make the metal get hotter and hotter and then it would stick together. The car would break down. We stop this happening by using oil to make the metal surfaces slippy. If you have a bike, it is friction that makes you go (tyre against road surface) and stop (brake pad against wheel rim).

We know that friction is caused by two surfaces gripping each other as they move over each other. Now think of the things that would work to increase friction, that is, to make more friction. If the football was covered in sandpaper, or fur, what effect would that have on how far the ball moved over the grass? Footballs are full of air. What if the ball was full of water, or lead? Would that make any difference to how far the ball moved? If we had a cardboard box full of picnic things and we had to push it along the grass, why would it be hard to push?

Questioning texts

Read a paragraph from *Worksheet 12B*, then talk together to
decide what your group thinks or understands about the text.
Write your answers down, then move on to the next paragraph.

Paragraph number: ___

Are there any words that must be looked up in the dictionary?

_____

What are three 'key words' for this paragraph?

_____

Can you write a summary of the paragraph?

_____

Two questions that this paragraph would answer are:

1.

_____

2.

_____

Looking into poems

Resources
Worksheet 13A: Looking into poems ; Worksheet 13B: Three short poems (or you could supply your own poems here).

Aims
To encourage children to justify opinions with reasons. To be able to arrive at a group decision. To deepen their understanding and appreciation of poetry.

Introduction
Explain to the children the aims for Lesson 13. Briefly remind the children of their chosen ground rules for group work. Give each group a copy of *Worksheets 13A* and *13B*. Explain that *Worksheet 13A* has some starter phrases for joint verbal criticism of the poems. Choose some children to read aloud the three poems, which will be used in the group activity.

Group work
Groups will take a poem at a time and discuss its content, form and written quality. The aim of this discussion is to come to an agreement about which piece is the group's favourite, which they like least, and why.

Plenary
Either: 1. Take one poem at a time, and ask groups what they enjoyed or disliked about it. Choose a class favourite poem for display.

Or: 2. Ask a group at a time to report on their discussion of any one poem. Display the poems, along with the reasons the children have given for liking or disliking them.

Restate the lesson aims and discuss whether children feel that these have been achieved.

Follow-up work

Ask the children to choose a poem each. In their talk groups, they should look at each poem in turn, together, stating what they like about the poems and why, without having to agree on a group favourite.

Poems could be displayed with comments, e.g. 'I liked this poem because . . .' or 'I did not like this poem because . . .'

Other lessons

1. The structure, language and content of a single poem can be the topic for group discussion. Instead of personal opinion, groups can discuss aspects of the poem, for example: rhyme scheme; the way words are used in phrases; subject; tone. The ground rules will enable all children to join in the discussion.

2. A class story could be the subject of discussion, using this structure. Groups could discuss their favourite character; their favourite episode in the story; whether they preferred reading the story or watching a TV/video version; their favourite type or genre of story. The emphasis should be on using the ground rules to support such discussion.

Looking into poems

Firstly, remind each other of the ground rules for talk. Now use the ground rules to help make a group decision about the poems.

Which poem did people like best?
Make sure everyone has a chance to state a favourite poem. Make sure everyone is asked why.

Look at the first poem
What is it about? Does it have any words or phrases that you like? Is there anything hard to understand about it? Is it funny or clever or interesting – why?
Make sure everyone has given an opinion. Can you sort out any difficult bits of the poem by talking together?

Look at the second poem
Do you like it more, or less than the first? Why? Has looking more carefully at the poem made anyone change his/her mind – why?

Look at the third poem
Do you like it more or less than the first and second poem – why? Has looking more carefully at the poem made anyone change his/her mind – why?

Decide on a group favourite poem
Talk together to decide which poem your group liked best. Make sure everyone is asked to talk. Ask everyone to give reasons for this choice. Keep talking until you have made a group decision that everyone agrees with!

Three short poems

Open All the Cages

Open all the cages,
Let the parrots fly –
Green and gold and purple parrots
Streaming up the sky.

Open all the cages,
Let the parrots out
Screeching, squawking
                parrots swooping
Happily about.

Open all the cages,
Set the parrots free –
Flocks of parrots
                flapping homewards
South across the sea.

Silent trees in silent forests
Long for parrots, so –
Open all the cages,
Let the parrots go!

© Richard Edwards from *Moon Frog*
(Walker Books)

I Have This Crazy Problem

When I was young
About six years old I wanted a dog.
I asked my Mum and Dad
to buy me a dog but all the time
they would say no.
So from then onwards
I started to steal dogs.
I would get a dog or two a day.
Now I am twenty-five years old and
I have collected
about five hundred dogs.

by Mohammed Khan

The Sea

The sea is a hungry dog,
Giant and grey.
He rolls on the beach all day.
With his clashing teeth and shaggy jaws
Hour upon hour he gnaws
The rumbling, tumbling stones,
And 'Bones, bones, bones, bones!'
The giant sea-dog moans,
Licking his greasy paws.

And when the night wind roars
And the moon rocks in the stormy cloud,
He bounds to his feet and sniffs and sniffs,
Shaking his wet sides over the cliffs,
And howls and hollos long and loud.

But on quiet days in May or June,
When even the grasses on the dune
Play no more their reedy tune,
With his head between his paws
He lies on the sandy shores,
So quiet, so quiet he scarcely snores.

©James Reeves, from *Complete Poems
for Children* (Heinemann) Reprinted by
permission of the James Reeves estate

Staying friends

Resources
Worksheet 14: a story – 'Staying Friends' (one copy per group).

Aims
To apply the ground rules to discussing social and moral choices. To deepen understanding of two citizenship issues: personal morality and bullying.

Introduction
Explain to the children the aims for Lesson 14. Choose fluent readers to read a paragraph each of the story aloud.

Group work
When the class has heard the story, ask the groups to discuss a story ending together, using their agreed ground rules for talk. They should consider:

▲ What sort of person is Joe/Abi/Charlie/Lucas?
▲ What choices does Charlie have at this point in the story?
▲ What would be the best thing to do – does Charlie do the best thing?
▲ Is Lucas a boy or girl – how do you know?

The discussions should take five to ten minutes. Once groups are ready, they can record their story ending in words or pictures.

Plenary
Each group reads out their story ending, giving reasons for their choices. Groups should be asked to say a little about their 'group dynamics': were the ground rules for talk used? If so, did they help everyone to feel they had taken part in a fair discussion? If not, what were the reasons for this? Restate the lesson aims and discuss with children whether they feel that these have been achieved.

Follow-up work

1. The class can further discuss the citizenship issues raised by the story, giving opinions on topics such as:

▲ friendship
▲ keeping secrets
▲ what is 'right' and 'wrong'
▲ why people choose to do things that they know are 'wrong'
▲ bullying – girls and boys.

2. The children could present and display their stories in written/cartoon form, or act out the entire story as a play.

Staying friends

Charlie, Abi and Joe did everything together. They were best friends, and everyone knew they were. Charlie and Joe got together one day to talk about what they were going to give Abi for her birthday. It was break time at school, so they only had a few moments to talk before Abi came along.

'I've already got Abi a present, but it's a secret,' said Joe. 'What is it?' asked Charlie. 'Go on, you can tell me.' 'But it's a secret,' Joe repeated. 'You know, something you don't tell anybody.' 'Huh, you can tell your friends secrets,' said Charlie. 'That's the point of having friends. People you can trust. I bet you haven't got a present at all, that's why you won't tell.' 'I have! So there,' said Joe, 'but . . .' 'I know, I know. It's a big secret. Well. I've got a secret too, and I won't tell it you unless you tell me about the present,' said Charlie, a bit crossly. 'Well,' said Joe reluctantly, 'you must promise not to tell. It's important to me. I'm not sure you've got a secret at all.' But Charlie had. 'That's all you know,' said Charlie. 'Listen, I promise. I'll tell mine first. And you promise too.' 'I promise,' said Joe, giving in.

'I've got a packet of sweets in my coat pocket!' whispered Charlie. That certainly was a secret, because no one was allowed sweets in school. Charlie proved it by showing Joe a corner of the packet. 'I'm going to eat them at lunchtime. You can share.' 'No! You idiot. You'll get into trouble.' 'Not a chance. I'm going to go right in the corner of the field. The dinner ladies never go that far.' 'You're crazy then,' Joe told him. 'Someone's bound to tell on you. Not me, I mean, because I promised. But someone will see you, and I bet they'll tell.' Charlie shrugged. 'I can get away with it, easy. Hey, now your turn – you have to tell me what you've got for Abi.' 'Oh, all right, then,' said Joe. He leaned closer and whispered, 'An electronic buzzer for her bike!' 'Wow,' said Charlie. Then they saw Abi running across the playground towards them, and they quickly started a game of tag.

Charlie's plan for lunchtime was to take a book and pretend to read in the corner of the field. Everyone would think he didn't want to be disturbed, and he could munch away quite happily behind the cover. It worked really well, and he'd eaten most of the sweets, when he was annoyed to spot Abi running across the field towards him. 'What's up with you?' she called. 'Go away! Can't you see I'm trying to read in peace?' he called back, but she came over and he hastily stuffed the packet back into his pocket. 'What do you mean, trying to read? That's a joke – you have to be forced to pick up a book in the classroom,' she said. 'Well I've decided to try harder,' said Charlie. It didn't sound very convincing.

Abi took a good look at him. 'Hmmm,' she said. 'Your mouth is a sort of greeny-black colour. Anyone would think you were over here eating sweets!' She laughed and Charlie had to laugh too, in a guilty sort of way, and they both looked around to see who was nearby. But everyone else was playing football, doing cartwheels, or just running about. 'Are you going to tell on me?' 'Me?' said Abi. 'No. I can keep a secret.' Charlie held out the sweets for her to take one, but she shook her head. 'I can keep secrets too,' said Charlie. 'And I know something you don't know.' 'Oh be quiet,' said Abi. 'You always think you know everything. You shouldn't be such a show off.' 'Well I do know something, so there, and it's about you, clever clogs.' Abi was a bit surprised by this, and quite interested. 'Go on, tell me then,' she said. 'It's a secret – I promised not to.' Charlie replied. 'See. You're just making things up as usual.' Charlie got quite cross again. 'If you must know, it's about your birthday,' he said. 'Joe told me what present he got you.' Abi smiled, and got up to go. 'You definitely mustn't tell me then. I love surprises! I'm off – I don't want to be in trouble like you. '

She ran away, and Charlie stuffed four of the sweets into his mouth and chewed hard. Somehow it didn't seem so much fun. And then, suddenly, from nowhere it seemed, Lucas Jones appeared beside him. Lucas had a horrible expression, a mixture of being pleased and very, very mean. 'Hello there Charlie. Enjoying your book?' said Lucas, sitting down, far too close. Charlie's mouth was too full to answer, but it didn't matter because he didn't know what to say anyway. He felt a wild, panicky feeling. He would have liked to run away, but where to, with a sticky, chewy mouthful of sweets? '

'Going to share them with me? Then I might not tell.' Lucas laughed nastily. Charlie dug hopelessly in his pocket and came out with the empty packet. 'Gone,' he mumbled, trying to swallow.

'I'd better tell, then,' said Lucas. 'Miss!' The dinner lady didn't seem to hear. Charlie dragged on Lucas's arm, imagining what would happen at home if he were caught. 'Shhh! Don't tell. Don't,' said Charlie. 'Why not? Got any money? No? Anything else? I might be very kind and not tell, but then what are you going to give me in return, hey?' Lucas managed to look even more unpleasant. 'I know – what were you and Joe whispering about at break? I saw you. You'd better tell me,' pinching Charlie's arm, 'I bet it was something about me.' 'Don't be daft,' said Charlie, wishing all of a sudden that the dinner lady were nearer. 'He was telling me about his new computer game.' Lucas hit him once, hard. 'Liar. Tell me. Or I'll tell on you. This is your last chance.' 'I can't tell; it was a secret, and I promised,' said Charlie in a panic. Why didn't the bell go? What could he say next? What would happen now?

Strategy

Resources
1cm-squared paper, pencils, rubbers, ruler, one counter/coin per group; Hurkle software on the *Thinking Together* website (optional)

Aims
To encourage collaboration in pairs. To accept group responsibility for decisions. To introduce and work with grid references or co-ordinates. To apply the ground rules to problem-solving in mathematics.

Introduction
Explain that children are paired to work with others in fours. Explain the grid system or the co-ordinate system that will be used. Introduce the version of the game you are using, stressing that the point is to talk together in order to discover the best strategy for finding the Hurkle, in as few goes as possible.

Group work
Children are paired. Each pair draws two grids on squared paper. The grids have the letters A to J along the bottom and the numbers 1 to 10 along the left-hand side. (If you want to use this to introduce co-ordinate work use numbers on both axes and ask them to refer to the bottom as horizontal or 'x' and the left side as vertical or 'y'.) To prepare for play, one member of each pair must first position their counter (or 'Hurkle') on one grid. This completed grid must be kept hidden.

Each pair then has to try to find the Hurkle by guessing which square it is in. Each pair starts with a blank grid and their own completed grid. Toss a coin to decide which pair starts. The starting pair decides on and chooses a square using conventional grid referencing, e.g., square G8. The opposing team has to reveal whether the Hurkle is in that square or not and add the following information:

Version 1: how far away the Hurkle is, counting each square up or along sideways as one square;

Version 2: whether the Hurkle is/is not within three squares of the guessed square;

Version 3: the direction that the Hurkle is to be found in, assuming the top of the grid to be North, the right-hand East, and so on. Double references e.g. NE or SW are only to be given if the Hurkle is directly diagonal to the guessed square.

Play the game enough times for the children to experiment with strategies; at least three times or more, depending on how much time you have available.

Plenary

Ask the groups of four which strategy they found worked the best, and to explain why to the class, using a large grid drawn on a blackboard or whiteboard. Ask for comments and discussion. The teacher should attempt to draw out the mathematical elements involved. In each version there is an optimum strategy and in each version it is different:

In Version 1: the optimum strategy is to guess two different points and then work out the intersections of the two circles which centre on each point, and have a radius of the distance given at each point.

In Version 2: it is to design a search pattern, keeping three squares from the edge and three squares from the last guess. Once within the area, three squares from the Hurkle, it is necessary to then draw an imaginary circle of possible squares, (three around the near guess) avoiding any squares within three squares of previous failed guesses, and then select a square within the designated area and repeat this procedure.

In Version 3: a good strategy is to start in a middle square, draw an imaginary line from the guessed square to the edge of the grid in the direction given, then place the next guess counter exactly half-way along this line. This strategy can be repeated indefinitely. The children may discover alternative strategies, using this version.

Finally, restate the lesson aims and discuss whether children feel that these have been achieved.

Follow-up work

▲ Children can prepare grids to use with someone at home.
▲ This lesson could be followed by work on adding and subtracting co-ordinates.

Other lessons

Other games can be played collaboratively, in order to help children work as a team, and minimise the conflict brought about by assigning 'blame' to individuals when things go wrong. Computer-based adventure programmes may also be useful when approached in this way. Draughts, dominoes, and other board games, which involve an element of choice as well as chance, can be used to support collaborative discussion between pairs of children.

Making a meaning web

> **Note:** For children's security, please ensure that all email sent and received is monitored. Do not allow children to send their home addresses or personal photographs.

Using computer-mediated communication (CMC)

Communication through computers such as email, bulletin boards and conferencing can support the same types of learning conversations that are found in face-to-face talk. However, it is unlikely that children will have spent as much time becoming adept in the use of computer-mediated communication as they will in learning to talk. Children may require further communication skills that have not been taught in the lessons in this book, such as keyboard skills and using email. It is unreasonable to expect children to apply all the ground rules for talk immediately in the new context of computer-mediated communication. That is why this lesson does not have the same format as previous lessons in this section. It proposes a flexible project that could stretch over a term or more, beginning with exercises to establish communication and to develop the face-to-face communication skills introduced in Section A.

Resources

The facility to send and receive email; a class of 'virtual friends' – that is, a class in another school who can be contacted regularly by email (see end of this lesson for suggestions on how to achieve this); multimedia authoring tools (optional).

Aims

To encourage educational co-operation between children. To enable children to share relevant information. To enable children to use technology as a communication tool.

Background work: getting to know each other

1. Explain to the children the aims for Lesson 16. Gather information about the children for their first contact with their virtual friends. First, each child must use the computer to write a brief note with some information about themselves, e.g. name; likes/dislikes; things they are good at; ambitions; favourite joke, etc. These notes can be collected in a single file to send when ready. The class must also prepare a brief description of their school, and their immediate location, perhaps providing map references. The current topics that are being studied could also be described.

2. First contact is made between the classes. The introductory messages are exchanged and read.

3. Both classes choose a 'class representative' to send off to each other. This could be a toy cat, mouse, snake – anything which can take on a personality and is light enough not to cost too much to post. The class gives their class representative a name and posts it off, or asks someone to deliver it in person. The partner class sends an email to report the safe arrival of the representative.

The purpose of the class representative is to give both classes a shared focus and theme for their communications. It can be taken on class outings, which could then be described to the partner class. It could also be given a 'voice' of its own in email communications. It could visit individual homes and report back, or talk about the weather or seasonal festivals. It might even get homesick. It could support effective group talk. At the end of the agreed project time, class representatives are sent home.

Sharing information: two projects

Where are we?
Groups are allocated partner groups in the other school. Each group must choose to describe one of the following to their partner group:

the ground plan of their own school;
one elevation of their own school.

The aim of the description is to enable the partner group to draw the plan or elevation, using only the written description. Descriptions should be composed by the group and then sent by email. Partner groups can ask questions via email to clarify any points they wish.

When the drawings are complete, they are scanned and sent to the partner school. The partner school then sends an actual plan, elevation, or photograph. Children can compare their drawings with the actual school, and comment on the accuracy of the descriptions they were given.

Topic web
Select a topic of mutual interest to the classes. The example used here is 'The Arctic.'

Task 1: Planning the web
Ask groups to draw a topic web. Children should talk together to decide what they might find out about by studying the topic (see the example on *Teacher information sheet 16*). Groups email their ideas for topics on the topic web to one another. Both classes should eventually agree on a 'complete web', which collates all the ideas from groups in both schools.

Task 2: Choosing a topic
Each group now discusses which topic on the complete web it would like to find out more about. Groups within the class should all be encouraged to tackle something different. Each group is then paired with a group in the partner school to study their joint topic.

Task 3: Information sheet

Children work in their groups to prepare a draft information sheet on the topic, to email to their partner group. Information can be collected from books, CD-ROMs, magazines and the Internet. The information sheet should be a definite length (1000 words maximum suggested). It can include references to web pages. This process could have a short time limit or can take place over a school term. Finished documents could be displayed and explained to the class by the group.

Task 4: Multimedia

If you have the appropriate equipment, children can produce and share multimedia web documents. These documents can be created using many word-processing packages such as Word 95 or 98 (you will need to create the pages and save as html), and also web-browsers such as Netscape and Explorer. A multimedia document includes images, which can be saved from CD-ROMs and the web, taken as photographs on digital cameras or scanned in from books and magazines, if you have a scanner. A multimedia document can also include sounds recorded by the children, and short clips of video recordings. You will need to check that these multimedia documents can be saved as attachments to emails and sent successfully between the schools. The easiest way to share them is as a file in html format on a web-server, where the partner school can read them using a web-browser and download them if they wish. Working in this way with partner schools, you can turn the initial concept map into a website with text, pictures and sounds.

To see an example of the way in which one middle school uses the web to display the results of projects, try:
http://www.heronsgate.milton-keynes.sch.uk/

Task 5: Quiz

Each group compiles a list of five questions about their own topic. The class makes a list of all the questions. Classes then exchange lists. The questions are tackled by children in their groups, and the partner class can 'mark' the answers.

Task 6: Evaluation

Groups should be asked to evaluate the 'topic web' project in terms of its success as a collaborative exercise. They could ask the following questions: What were the advantages of working in a group with classmates? What were the disadvantages? How could these problems be solved? What were the advantages of discussing information with the partner class? What were the disadvantages? How could these problems be solved? How well did the technology support group work in class/at a distance? Which information was most memorable? Why?

Email project partners can be found at the following web addresses:

1. Curriculum projects using the Internet, organised by the British Council (Australia) with the Central Bureau for Educational Visits and Exchanges, UK. **http://www.bc.org.au/montage**

2. Educational links to enable pupils to complete design projects together; organised by the Design Council with the Central Bureau for Educational Visits and Exchanges. **http://www.designit.org**

3. Find partners for collaborative projects in Europe: European SchoolNet **http://www.eun.org**

4. Windows on the world: school links set up by The Central Bureau for Educational Visits and Exchanges to promote international projects. This has a School Gates database, which can help teachers find project partners. **http://www.wotw.org.uk**

5. Links to UK schools **http://www.eyesoftime.com/teacher/ukpage.htm**

6. Virtual Teachers Centre for links to other teachers **http://www.vtc.org.uk**

7. More links to other schools: Schools in Cyberspace **http://www.strath.ac.uk/~cjbs17/Cyberspace/index.html**

More information about
Thinking Together

Bibliography

The research on which *Thinking Together* is based is described in the following publications:

Neil Mercer (2000) *Words and Minds: How we use language to think together*. London: Routledge.

Neil Mercer, Rupert Wegerif and Lyn Dawes (1999) 'Children's talk and the development of reasoning in the classroom'. *British Educational Research Journal*. 25 (1): 95-111.

Rupert Wegerif, Neil Mercer and Lyn Dawes (1999) 'From social interaction to individual reasoning: an empirical investigation of a possible socio-cultural model of cognitive development'. *Learning and Instruction*. 9(5): 493-516.

Elizabeth Grugeon, Lorraine Hubbard, Carol Smith, and Lyn Dawes (1998) *Teaching speaking and listening in the primary school*. London: David Fulton.

Rupert Wegerif, Neil Mercer and Lyn Dawes (1998) 'Software design to support discussion in the primary classroom'. *Journal of Computer Assisted Learning*. 14(3): 199-211. ISSN:-0260-4909.

Rupert Wegerif and Lyn Dawes (1998) 'Encouraging exploratory talk around computers'. In M. Monteith (Ed) *IT for Learning Enhancement*. Exeter: Intellect Press.

Rupert Wegerif and Peter Scrimshaw (Eds.) (1997) *Computers and talk in the primary classroom*. Clevedon: Multilingual Matters.

Neil Mercer (1995) *The guided construction of knowledge: talk amongst teachers and learners*. Clevedon: Multilingual Matters.

Further details and the full text of some research articles can be found on the *Thinking Together* website:

http://www.thinkingtogether.org.uk

Children's certificate

A certificate is a good means of emphasising to children what they have achieved in their efforts to talk and think together. A suggested format appears opposite. However, the children might also like to design their own.

> Don't forget that you can access the *Thinking Together* website at the following address:
>
> http://www.thinkingtogether.org.uk

Talk Lesson Certificate

This is to certify that

_____

has been part of a talk group
and learnt how to discuss
before deciding.

Members of my group:

Talk Lesson Certificate

This is to certify that

_____

has been part of a talk group
and learnt how to discuss
before deciding.

Members of my group: